Joan Bakewell has had a fifty year career in broadcasting and is still at it. Born in Stockport, graduated in Cambridge, she has published an autobiography, *The Centre of the Bed*, and two novels: *All the Nice Girls* and *She's Leaving Home*. She has two children, six grandchildren, and sits in the House of Lords as a Labour Peer. She lives in North London.

'[Joan Bakewell's] new book is a joy'   *Psychologies*

'She has lost none of her intellectual curiosity'
                                        Bee Wilson, *Sunday Times*

'Companionable and insightful . . . by turns entertaining, frank and – when dealing with death and loss – unflinching. It is, then, true to the spirit of a most accomplished woman, who has always had the knack of making whatever she does look easy. When it comes to facing down old age with such style and honesty, that is perhaps the most impressive achievement of all'   *Herald*

'What makes Bakewell so thoroughly engaging is her ongoing thirst for knowledge . . . Bakewell has added an elegant and elegiac pause to the many things already left behind'
                                        Cary Gee, *Tribune*

STOP THE CLOCKS

Thoughts on What I Leave Behind

JOAN BAKEWELL

virago

VIRAGO

First published in Great Britain in 2016 by Virago Press
This paperback edition published in 2017 by Virago Press

1 3 5 7 9 10 8 6 4 2

A CIP catalogue record for this book
is available from the British Library.

ISBN 978-0-349-00611-6

Typeset in Perpetua by M Rules
Printed and bound in Great Britain by
Clays Ltd, St Ives plc

Papers used by Virago are from well-managed forests
and other responsible sources.

Virago Press
An imprint of Little, Brown
Carmelite House
50 Victoria Embankment
London EC4Y 0DZ

An Hachette UK Company
www.hachette.co.uk

www.virago.co.uk

To those who follow after —
Harriet, Andy, Matthew, Sally,

and after them —
Thomas, Louis, Katie, Max, Charlie, Maisie

CONTENTS

Prologue

I am one of the oldest people I know. My generation is dying off, moving over to make way for the next. When we are gone there will be no one who remembers what it felt like to live through the second half of the last century. Every day there are fewer and fewer witnesses.

That is why I am writing this book. I want to look back at the world that shaped me and look forward to what the next generation will inherit. Theirs is a very different world from mine and is already beginning to feel strange.

Right now I still feel very much alive. Each day is just as vivid and precious as it always was. I may be further along the country lane than those who follow after but the sunshine is just as golden, the flowers as bright. The last strawberry in the dish tastes as good as the first.

But the decades don't roll out ahead of me as they did when I was younger. I can't stop the clocks, no matter how much I'd like to. Instead I roam around the decades and experiences of my life, exploring memories both trivial and important that have come to seem precious.

On Beginning

In the middle of old age I find myself in a small cottage.

No more than two rooms: a latch opens the door into a tiny entrance then directly into the lower room. Nothing between, no preparation for arriving. Just straight into the one room – there is no other. This is for eating, working, living. Enough and immediate. Life is full of transition. What we need is to get stuck in. So, open the door and come in.

Inside is the creation of a woman of country taste, a woman who obviously takes time, who pays attention to detail, who is not in a hurry. The room is no bigger than a small study. And that's exactly what it is. Along one wall extend all the facilities a writer needs: a desk, rows of electrical sockets, a laptop, a CD player and radio, a television set, a router and a printer. This working space is tucked beneath the slope of the stairs, which in turn supports a set of narrow shelves for paperclips, stationery, a jar of pens, a torch. It is all I need.

Central to the same room is an elegant round table and two Edwardian chairs. And beyond, a series of cupboards with pine doors and drawers that open to reveal a fridge, pots and pans, tablecloths, rolls of silver foil . . . the active equipment of good and easy cooking. Walls front and back have leaded windows opening onto beds of daffodils: crowded below, a comfy sofa, cushions, standard lamp, all nudging up to a small wood-burning stove and a display of sepia family photographs. The whole is an exercise in minimal space with all anyone could need. And if it has a feel of Mrs Tiggy-Winkle about it that's appropriate because in the single upstairs room is a full set of Beatrix Potter's little books, their box set cunningly pinned to the wall of a large cupboard concealing a lavatory. Such economy of space leaves room for a large, tall and wide bed heaped with pillows and a duvet in the William Morris fabrics that feature elsewhere. Under the window is a free-standing bath.

Here I shall stay. Here I shall set out my pages, catch at memories, weigh my life against the future and pin down ideas about what I will leave behind. There won't be time for more.

I don't want this to be a book about ageing: I want it to be about life. The two are by no means incompatible, but ageing is often seen as a diminution of life, somehow a feeling of being less alive than in earlier years. The generation that sets the tone of contemporary thinking does so from a younger perspective: a perspective that infiltrates magazines and papers, advertising, programmes on television, films and sports. The way they move through life, shopping, working, pushing prams, going out with friends . . . gives them a single viewpoint – their own.

Being young, they use their imaginations to make assumptions about the old. They look around and see people who look wrinkly and stooped. Perhaps they get impatient with people who walk

The writer's cottage: Hosking Houses Trust

slowly. It's quite odd using the underground when you're my age because the general public moves at a brisk pace and I don't need to or want to. Some sort of group instinct takes over and sets the common rhythm, urgent, stressed, in a hurry to be wherever they're heading. I'm under no such pressure: I am happy to idle my way to where I'm going. I try not to catch their mood of urgency but it's quite hard to resist the pressure. I can tell they see me as old and tiresome, getting in the way, someone who would be living at their speed if I only could. But that's not the case at all. I am living the life of an old person, which has its own rhythms, its own priorities, its own satisfactions. They are not inferior, or declining. They are simply different.

The old are living through their own segment of the human lifespan, different but of equal significance. Shakespeare has done us no favours here. Writing *As You Like It* in his buoyant thirties he gave his personal take on the old. It was a subjective view from his position as lively and successful writer/actor, an outlook many of his audience would share. He clearly identified – you can sense it in the lines – with the sighing lover and the jealous soldier; he even hints at a sly admiration for the justice with his fair round belly. But mockery and lampoon follow – the lean and slippered pantaloon with his shrunk shank and childish treble of a voice. And finally despair: second childishness and mere oblivion. This is the voice of a virile, assertive and successful man, writing when life expectancies were much shorter than today and the old – Falstaff, Lear, even Prospero – are seen giving up on the triumphs they had known.

Many more of us reach old age today. And possibly because of our numbers, our health, our background we are not ready to fit easily into stereotypes. We need the old to write about being old, and indeed about dying so the young can know what it's like and not be fearful. One or two writers have tried. The playwright Dennis Potter talked to Melvyn Bragg about being close to death, swigging morphine to ease the pain throughout their television interview. He spoke lyrically of the beauty of cherry blossom outside his window, how it was more frothily white than he had ever appreciated. We held our breath with the courage of it all. Now it seems to us accurate as well. Oliver Sacks, the neurologist and author of outstanding books, was told he had terminal cancer at the age of eighty-one. He wrote of how that changed his outlook: 'I have been able to see my life as from a great altitude, as a sort of landscape, and with a deepening sense of the connection of all its parts . . . I feel a sudden clear focus and perspective. There is no time for anything inessential. I must focus on myself, my work and my friends.' That is what many of us are doing.

That is what I will try to do here. I have a sense of that landscape of which Oliver Sacks speaks.

Time: it has always haunted me.

When I walked to school, along the suburban pavements, under the dripping tunnels that carried the London to Manchester trains, past the greyhound track and the cinema towards the tram terminal, I would time myself exactly.

I needed to be at school three miles away by ten past nine. It therefore became a matter of whether I caught the 8.25 tram and felt comfortably able to walk the six minutes from the tram terminal to school, or the 8.27½ tram which I knew was cutting it fine and I would need to be relatively brisk to cover the same ground, or the 8.30 tram when I would twitch uneasily all the way on the swaying clanking tram in fear of being late and knowing I would have to half-trot my way to my destination. If this happened I would arrive breathless and anxious, change into my indoor shoes fast, fling my coat aslant onto its designated peg and walk as swiftly as I was allowed – running incurred bad marks – into the classroom, where my form mistress might already be reading the register. The calling of the register was the defining moment.

'Here, no!' we would answer as our names were called. This indicated not only that we were present and not liable for a late mark, but also that 'no' meant we had not left our purse or any money in the cloakroom. This again was a culpable offence and would add to other bad marks that might steadily mount up throughout the school day. My grammar-school education consisted not only of algebra and the Treaty of Utrecht, but a steady struggle to avoid the unrelenting judgement of those mounting marks.

I have feared censure ever since. The consistent and nagging disapproval that shadowed us set a pattern of expectation in me that there was no pleasing the powers that be. As an adult the idea still haunts me. And there is considerable evidence that it is so. I flinch every time I get a parking fine, the notice of congestion charge or council tax, the road tax renewal form, and even, now I am old, the postal vote for which I am registered. To fail to vote would in my eyes earn another conduct mark against my name.

Whole generations of children grew up knowing they were in the wrong. If not directly, then incipiently likely to offend some unknown rule imposed by others. It would take the arrival of child psychology and the ideas spread by the social sciences for things to change. They would begin to ask what made children happy, what helped them thrive . . . issues totally beyond the mindset of my parents' generation, who believed their job was to enforce the agreed rules, rules born of Christian commandments, large families in small spaces and aspirations to class respectability. It was how society instilled civilised behaviour in its children, behaviour that would translate them into obedient and conforming adults. The penalties of failing were too great.

Why then did I take risks? Why dice with the horrible option held out by the 8.30 tram when I could make all things smooth on the 8.27½? Even at the age of ten I was pushing what little freedom I had to the limit. I simply didn't want to play safe. I teased that tiny bit of risk out of my daily routine to give me some autonomy in a world that wanted to flatten me out. It constituted a small triumph.

Years later when I sat on the board of the National Theatre, we would meet promptly at 10 a.m. on the designated day. We enjoyed those meetings: we were conscious of the responsibility we had, and relished it; we enjoyed each other's company; we were people from different walks of life but in general terms schooled in problem solving; for an entire morning we focused on the theatre's destiny. There was one board member, however, who arrived on time . . . his time. At ten minutes past ten. You could set your watch by his arrival, which involved a mumbled apology which our chairman came to acknowledge with no more than a bleak smile. One day, as our friendship grew, I asked him privately, 'You are always ten minutes late. Why not set out ten minutes earlier and be sure to arrive on time?'

'Oh, I do,' he was eager to explain, 'I do, believe me, but even when I do I am still always ten minutes late.' I knew the case of an 8.30 tram when I met it.

I have caught many 8.30 trams in my time. Groomed by family and school to play safe, some inner impulse, some niggling devil persistently urged me to defy them. No one ever knew: such a tiny discrepancy was scarcely detectable to the adults. But I knew. And I stayed that way. I am like that today.

The trams of my schooldays were the workhorses of transport. Buses were more comfortable, not limited to the rigid lines in the road, and cost more. So I walked further to take the tram. To climb on board was to enter a whole noisy world of clatter and clang. The network that stretched out from Manchester and Stockport depended for power on each tram having a pole that fixed onto the power line above. I lived at the terminus and

The tram of my youth

no tram was turned round at its destination; they were simply switched back to front. The conductor went along the aisle slamming the wooden-slatted bench backs across to face the opposite direction. At the same time the driver would pull on the pole, which would flash and crackle as it left the power line and swung round from front to back to reconnect with the electricity. Then the tram would be off, swaying along the fixed tracks down the centre of the road, stopping to pick up passengers who would hold up what motor traffic there was – very little in those days – stepping out from the pavement to reach and mount the several steps onto the huge mechanical beast. On board they would pay the conductor, who dispensed individual tickets from a small board mounted with what seemed to be several mousetraps and made a hole with a primitive puncher slung round his neck. Each ticket carried a series of numbers and each day we would add and subtract them according to obscure childhood rules that indicated the future patterns of our fantasy love lives. Would the boy next door stop to speak? Would we bump into a pash at the Scouts' dance? Nowadays items such as these crop up in transport museums and on bric-a-brac stalls. There's no conveying what they once meant.

The journey to school was a kaleidoscope of excitement, hopes and fears, yearnings and terrors. Often, depending on the timing, the headmistress would get on the tram half way along the route: she would travel inside; we were upstairs. She was gaunt and watchful, eagle-eyed for any pupil not wearing the full school uniform or not quick enough to offer their seat when the tram was crowded. We kept a discreet distance. We did the same for the man upstairs, sitting in the curving seat at the back in full view as we clambered down the curving metal stairs. He regularly had a strange purple gizzardy-looking thing hanging from between his legs. We giggled together once we had jumped from the steps, but we weren't sure why. We were careful not to let the headmistress see.

Trams fell from favour in the post-war years. Manchester was the first city in Britain to abandon them, tearing up the lines almost with relish, rejecting the noisy old past. Then with just as much gusto they were back: arriving transformed, as though they'd just been away for a makeover. This time there was to be no clanging or flashing electricity. Instead a seemly smooth glide, and low floors so wheelchairs and prams can get on. Trams have been gentrified, first running in 1992 and given modish branding as the Manchester Metrolink. Casual talk of trams as I remember them falls on deaf ears . . . they don't remember. They don't want to know. It's their world now.

———

Edinburgh is an altogether different story. I have waited patiently and long while the protracted saga of its own tram system has been played out over some ten years. Each time I visited the Edinburgh Festival I enquired how it was getting along; groans and complaints from taxi drivers and frustrated burghers. Suddenly in May 2014 it is opened, at half the length and having taken twice as long as first intended. It had better be good.

It is mid-June: I arrive at Edinburgh airport in the tumultuous company of those involved in the making of a television programme. The star is led off by a peak-capped chauffeur to what we all imagine is a limousine. I demur: 'No, I want to take the tram.' Strange looks from the rest as they themselves bundle into a series of taxis. I make my way back into my past, back into tram-land . . . back to what I used to know and love. Some things change, and some things stay the same.

The tram is back, but this time the design is like something out of Bauhaus via the Wild West. The design is streamlined, the route still through rough terrain. The tram terminus lies in the usual wasteland of covered walkways that fringe all airports; there are not many passengers so we are easily accommodated in the crisp new carriages. So much money spent and they want us to be proud: 'We love our seats: please help us to keep them looking lovely by not putting your feet on them. Thanks.' The seats are not so much lovely as serviceable, but I smile at the newness and pride of it all.

The route towards Edinburgh takes us through the bush and shrublands of the city plain; for long stretches I can see nothing but grass. And then the tram slinks silently into a station of such elegance and style it should win design awards: signs, waste bins, rain shelters are all in the finest brushed steel, with minimalist taste and discretion. The doors hum open and one or two passengers arrive: where have they come from? There don't seem to be any houses for miles. Nearer to the city the shape of the future arrives: large warehouses and company buildings begin to line the track. They will soon, I imagine, spread out along the so-far-empty route. But for a moment I am enjoying the tram of today in all its isolated and surprising glory.

—

I close the cottage door behind me and turn towards the river down a small lane, really nothing more than an alley. A bicycle could get down here, but not a car. It has the air of a doll's-house settlement. Along one side there is a line of houses as small as the one I am living in. Each a front door and a single window. On their doorsteps a medley of pots with clusters of flowers and a sudden magnificent magnolia, a sequence of wooden fencing, a rackety wire-netting enclosure for a clutch of hens and a magnificent cockerel called Chanticleer.

Winding around small grassy spaces – different gardens, it's impossible to say whose – I reach the river and the bench. It is where I come to sit. And think about life, my life, and its steady flow like the river from its source towards its ceasing.

I watch the raindrops bounce their rings on its surface until I see so many rings I don't know how heavily it's raining. A tall old yew tree provides shelter. I watch the rain, the river and the banks. I can almost see the green buds bursting into leaf. All is in constant flux . . . as it has been all my life. Only now am I aware of it.

—

The tram of my age

I shall only know what I leave behind, if I realise what has gone into making me what I am. And the earliest years echo most vividly in my eighty-two-year-old memory.

I was born into a safe, stable world of industrial Lancashire, where my parents worked purposefully to make more of their lives than they had known at home. Both my grandfathers had been factory workers, working with their hands at jobs that didn't vary throughout their lives. Their regular but static wages paid the rent on small terraced houses with scarcely enough left to feed and clothe their numerous children. Several of these children were excited by how schooling could

The path through the gardens . . . to the River Avon

help them make something of their lives – it was called 'bettering yourself'. My parents were among them. It was to give them motivation and integrity; in furthering this intent they led straightforward, law-abiding lives.

For the most part my grandparents accepted the social order they knew, though living in the centre of Manchester they were well aware of its radical traditions. In 1819 an early meeting of Chartists had been mown down by mounted yeomanry in St Peter's Field; at the turn of the twentieth century the suffragettes had flourished locally and were grudgingly admired, even if they did irritate my grandparents' heroes Lloyd George and Winston Churchill.

But life was tough and several children died young. My father was bereaved early when his thirty-three-year-old father died, leaving a twenty-eight-year-old widow and four children under the age of six. My father was the eldest.

Misfortune was followed by good fortune: all three boys were taken in by Chetham's Hospital, an orphanage founded in the seventeenth century by the Manchester worthy Humphrey Chetham to provide by 'learning and labour' for forty boys, each the son of honest and industrious parents and not 'a bastard, nor lame, infirm nor diseased'. The deserving, as opposed to the undeserving, poor.

Here he received a rigorous and purposeful education – pupils were destined to be apprentices serving the city's industries. But 'Chet's', as it was known to parents and friends, also provided a glimpse of something else. Its fine library – the first public library in Europe – housed tall leather-bound volumes of law, theology and local history. My father grew up in awe of scholarship and learning. It was a direct inheritance into my own life and values, for which I am continually thankful.

My mother, the eldest daughter among eight children, was also keen to better her lot. She was bright enough to win a City of Manchester scholarship to Ardwick Central School but left after a year, aged thirteen, either because – family stories vary – the family couldn't afford the uniform and she minded the stigma, or because my perpetually pregnant grandmother needed help bringing up her brood. It was often the fate of the eldest daughter to be a second mother. But they needed money too. So my mother took a job in an engineering firm and enrolled in evening classes at Openshaw College, studying applied mechanics and experimental maths. It was the second year of the First World War and she was part of that wave of women offered interesting work by the absence of men. In the event she became a tracer, skilled at tracing with absolute accuracy the detailed engineering drawings drawn up by men. It was as high up the ladder as women could go.

Her intelligence and resentment were, I believe, to fuel the depressions that overtook her in later life, and her barely suppressed jealousy of the freedoms I enjoyed. But for the time being, following their office romance, my parents settled into the comfortable suburban life that had seemed so remote a dream for their parents. They were upwardly mobile and they thrived.

They believed in bringing up their children with high hopes and new thinking. I and my sister Susan were, they hoped, to benefit from the latest styles of childcare. They belonged to what must have been the first generation to take their child-rearing skills not, as if by osmosis, from their parents, but from the advice of strangers written in books.

With a background thick with time-keeping and bad marks for trivia I was clearly available for any chance to break out. I grew into a slyly subversive child. The point was to defy the system without the system really knowing. I could become sullen and obstinate simply for the sake of asserting myself. When I was five my father was sent to South America as an engineer working on the construction of wheat silos at the docksides of Argentina. My mother and I went along too. This was a big deal for people so aware of their humble background: they were thrilled to be travelling but self-conscious about things like correct etiquette and behaviour. My mother, who was pretty and popular, was naturally treated with Hispanic gallantry by my father's Argentinian colleagues. This made her even more self-conscious. High-flown manners did not come easily if you'd grown up in the land of L. S. Lowry. In response, my mother felt it her duty to enact the appearance of being perfect and of her family's being perfect too. That meant me.

There is a photograph of some 1930s moment of formal hospitality on board an ocean liner where everyone is smiling – with formal Argentinian manners – towards the camera. Except two people: my mother and I. She is standing above me in a grey squirrel fur coat, and looking down at me with disapproval: I know she is. But I am looking away from her, and defiantly refusing to look at the camera. We are locked in a tug of wills. I have offended by refusing to thank one of the ship's officers who has made me a present of a propelling pencil bearing the gilt lettering Royal Mail Lines, Ltd. My mother has taken the propelling pencil from me until such time as I thank the officer politely for his gift. I refuse. I went on refusing.

I went on refusing until her death twenty-three years later. Then in the muddle of dusty debris that lay scattered inside her dressing-table drawer I found the very pencil. I claimed it as mine. And I still have it. And some fifty years further on, now I have already outlived her by a quarter of a century, it sits along with other pencils and pens in a pot on my desk.

What to make of this tale? For years I saw it as a trophy, an early triumph in defying my mother. Now I see it also as an infantile tantrum whose impulse to defy authority has not yet died away in me. My mother and I never resolved our battle of wills. And I always blamed her for treating me in ways that were flawed and counterproductive. But don't all parents do that? Unresolved traumas like this curdled our later life together.

—

As I sit watching the rain has got heavier, the raindrops on the river merging into a continuously rippling surface. The buds seem more swollen than ever. I am impatient for the yellow of spring to arrive. I am hurrying time on. To what end? To my own. But how to slow down the flowers? I leave the bench. Time and the river have moved on. I go back up the path and inside for a cup of tea.

On Names

The path down to the river meanders between a patchwork of smallholdings, fenced-in stretches of land not directly attached to any house but known to their owners who tend and groom them, combining the preoccupied attention of the allotment holder with the more casual pleasures of the garden. Each day I wend my way down the narrow space between, stopping to enjoy. A sudden and surprising favourite is a field full of dandelions, nothing else, a carpet of yellow in full bloom every one. No other wild flowers . . . golden dandelions singing to the sun. I make it a morning rendezvous.

Yesterday I found the entire spread had been cut down, scythed deliberately; the implement left its mark. I was heart-broken. And yet I had known the dandelions only four days. And they would soon have turned to dandelion clocks anyway. But there was now no prospect of dandelion clocks in the little enclosure. Someone had preferred order to nature. It added sadness to my day.

What a lovely name: dandelion.

The name dandelion comes from the French *dent de lion*,

meaning lion's tooth, but it's also known as blowball, yellow-gowan, doon-head-clock, monks-head, priest's-crown and puff-ball. It evolved some thirty million years ago in Eurasia, and has been used by humans as food and as a herb for most of recorded history. I think it will survive a brutal scything in an English field.

Handing on the name to future generations is what the upper classes take seriously and everyone else does without thinking. Our name is a clear and evident legacy which we hand on willy-nilly through the family records that once used to be stored at Somerset House and are now digitised and kept somewhere obscure. It is of course far more complicated than that. And it is getting even more so.

I have standing behind me ranks of Welsh ancestors proudly boasting the name Rowlands. So proud are they, they often double it up: say it with a Welsh lilt in your voice and it sounds like a Dylan Thomas play.

My great-great-grandfather was Thomas Rowlands, father of Roland Thomas Rowlands, who begat John Morgan Rowlands, whose son John Roland Rowlands was my father. As if to make the point yet more forcefully Rowlands isn't enough: it has to be Roland as well that is passed down the ages. They simply couldn't get enough of this Rowlands/Roland business, whatever it signifies. It is as though they want to etch it on every wall, inscribe it on every document, roll it out on their tongue at every meeting with strangers, and naturally, at the end, leave it to gather moss and lichen on a tombstone. I in my turn have kept up the tradition: my son has the name John, and his son is Thomas Roland.

I set out to track it down: if I am at the end of a long line I would like to know where it begins. Many people feel the same. The television series *Who Do You Think You Are?* prompts audiences to ask this of themselves. I knew the idea would be popular when I first suggested it to the BBC many years ago: they ascribed me a producer/researcher to see whether we could develop it. But every idea we came up with was made of paper: parish registers, births, marriages and deaths entries, wills and family legal documents ... the evidence piled high. But you can't make a programme only of paper. The project ran into the ground. Then the years rolled by and the concept of celebrity was invented. Celebrity was exactly what such a programme needed. It was not me but someone else entirely who had this new idea and made a success of it. But even today celebrity isn't enough – even modest celebrity. Television needs narrative and one that is spiced with either scandal or surprises. A bit of skulduggery goes down well; unexpected links across frontiers give an episode an exotic setting. When the researcher came round to test out my Rowlands background I asked her to turn up some dashing Welsh pirate I could celebrate. With regret, she came back with nothing exciting at all, merely a long line of solemn Welshmen and women living modest lives as gardeners and shop folk in Aberystwyth. The nearest we came to a Welsh pirate was a Rowlands who worked in the customs house when Aberystwyth was a busy port trading iron ore with Spain. The wrong side of the law altogether. So the programme was never made. No doubt the research was filed and shelved under the label 'Too Dull to Tell'. 'Don't worry,' she comforted me. She could tell I was downcast at not having glamorous antecedents. 'It happens to lots of people we investigate: David Frost's family is like that too.'

So here's what the paper record tells me about Rowlands. One source says it derives from the Norman-French name Rollant, made up of a seventh-century German root 'Hrdo', meaning 'renown', and ' land', meaning . . . well . . . land. The name was quite popular during the Middle Ages because one of Charlemagne's knights commander bore it. Then it came over with the Conquest. Another source says it derives from the Norse word 'ra', meaning deer or roebuck, and 'lundr', meaning a wood, and was associated with places in Sussex and Derbyshire. I am moved by both these explanations, allowing my imagination to drift towards armoured knights riding fast horses across Europe's northern plains or seeking the lyrical shade of English woodlands and the shy glimpse of passing deer. I am happy to settle for Joan Deerpark.

The other side of the family – the maternal line – has of course been subsumed into the male. My mother's mother was a Dawson, who married Grandfather Bland. The Blands were a Midlands family, my grandfather Bill Bland working as a cooper in a brewery as had his father, grandfather and great-grandfather before him. Not much social mobility there then. But it was a secure respectable artisan trade passed easily down the generations, with the Coopers' Society finding work for its members whenever times were slack. In 1903 when cooperage jobs were squeezed in Wolverhampton, the society found work for my grandfather at Ardwick Brewery in Manchester, and the family moved north. Of my grandmother's Dawson line little fuss was made, though the shadowy names of several aunts drifted through my childhood. Out of traditional loyalty, mother to daughter, I was given Dawson as my middle name. Decades later the then chairman of the BBC Trust Sir Christopher Bland used to hail me as 'cousin' in the fond belief that all those with the same name must, somewhere in the mix and however remotely, be related.

Except that neither Bland, Dawson nor Rowlands is the name by which I am known. As a woman married in the 1950s there was no question but that I would take my husband's name. I had passed from my father's care and name into that of my husband. It was what women of my class did. Women of other classes, where issues of inheritance obtained, were happy to combine their name with that of their husband for the sake of preserving the name and the inheritance.

The double-barrelled surname has become the way women in Britain have found to declare both their own identity and their married status. But with women's increasing assertiveness the shift in names is accelerating. Facebook's research conducted for the *Sunday Times* found that 62 per cent of women in their twenties took their husband's name and 74 per cent of those in their thirties did so, compared with 88 per cent of those in their sixties. Hyphenating names – your own with your husband's – is less common: 3 per cent of those in their sixties did so, 6 per cent in their 30s, 4 per cent in their twenties. What names will these women be passing on to their children and thence their grandchildren? If the child of the Chaddington-Smythes marries one of the Miller-Hopkins, what will happen? Within a couple of generations you could build up a string of names too long to get on a passport. The proportion of unmarried mothers adds to the complexity. Mothers with children by different fathers presumably pass on their own surname, thus confusing the paternal line for the next generation. The question 'Who do you think you are?' may have more poignant issues of identity than a television programme can bear.

I seriously believe an 'n' and an 'a' could have made my life different. If I had been called Joanna rather than Joan I would have felt altogether different about myself and so would the world. How did Joan come about? My mother, who was herself called Rose, knew too many people whose names have been shortened or distorted; it worried her. She had an Aunt Harriet who was known as Hetty, and a relation christened Mary and known as Polly. She didn't like it. She felt there was little over which she had control: a crowded terrace home in Gorton (think *Coronation Street*), loads of siblings, off to work at thirteen. As she grew up she came to feel very possessive about decisions she was making for herself. My name was one of them. It was also the case that among the film stars in the ascendant at that time were Joan Crawford and Joan Bennett.

Strangely, Joan Crawford was born Lucille Fay LeSueur. So someone actually thought you had a better chance of fame and fortune if you opted for Joan. According to her biographer, it

Another Joan . . . Joan Bennett

was a name selected for her by her fans in a studio-sponsored competition. It is a quaint reflection on shifting taste that today Lucille LeSueur would be an instant brand of exotic glamour, which is what the poor little girl from San Antonio always hankered for. As Joan she made every effort to make her name in the sleazy world of 1930s Hollywood using every skill she had, most in demand being her sexual availability and invention that led many men to her bed. She had a sequence of unmemorable husbands, and affairs with Clark Gable and Spencer Tracy. She gave a great performance in *Mildred Pierce* but became legendary with the role of the crazed sister of Bette Davis in *What Ever Happened to Baby Jane?* Her stardom was worldwide, and must certainly have reached a modest cinema in Manchester in the years when my father was courting my mother.

Joan Bennett seems to have been less neurotic, if only because she was too busy working her way through a career of some seventy movies: Joan was the name her parents gave her, and although she didn't change her name for the sake of stardom she did change her appearance. She was a natural and lively blonde until the 1930s when her then husband, the director Walter Wanger, persuaded her to go brunette and take on an altogether more sultry persona. Perhaps it was the dark hair, among other things, that got her shortlisted for the part of Scarlett O'Hara in 1938. If it was these actress Joans who swayed my parents, it certainly wasn't Shakespeare.

Shakespeare has not dealt generously with Joan. It was the name of his elder sister who had died before his birth. His parents then went on to give a subsequent child the same name: they must have liked it a good deal to pass it from a dead child to a living. So this second Joan was William's younger sister. It was to her he left twenty pounds in his will, along with the right to live in the western part of the family house in Henley Street for the nominal rent of a shilling a year. You might have expected, in view of this, some tenderness towards the name. But perhaps the most conspicuous Joan in Shakespeare's plays brought me nothing but grief. *Love's Labour's Lost* was not a play we studied at school but its poem 'Winter' was much anthologised and we embarked on a line-by-line analysis. The refrain hit home: 'While greasy Joan doth keel the pot'. The class erupted in those waves of giggles that have the irritating hum of trying to be stifled. I didn't know what to do. I clearly couldn't join the giggles because they and the glances from round the room were directed at me. I imagine I simply stared at my book and slowly blushed in the way that girls do, from the neck rising to flame fully across the cheeks. I certainly didn't yield or cry or flee, and it being that sort of school the English mistress would soon have called for order and threatened any further giggling or the girl will be sent out. Being sent out was a major risk, for one might be spotted by the headmistress cruising the corridors for just such delinquents.

Greasy Joan, we learned once the hubbub had subsided, was a reference to a servant working in the kitchens and keeling the pot meant keeping it from boiling over by adding cooler liquid. This explanation didn't improve things at all. I had been named after the lowest skivvy. Had she known this, my mother, who had the aspirations of the lower working class, would have been mortified. Her reaction would have had the logic of her temperament: she would have blamed my humiliation on Shakespeare himself.

Joan has fallen out of fashion now. It dates me to a specific era, just as much as Mildred, Ethel, Muriel and Fanny. But it never occurred to me to alter it. How would that be possible? It was enshrined on my birth certificate, and on my baptism card. It had the irrevocable power of state and church: who was I to challenge it? In those days it was simply not acceptable for families like mine to tamper with authority.

Things are different now ... People change their names all the time. And given the wild and silly names celebrities inflict on their children it's perhaps as well they won't suffer qualms about it. But it does make me wonder what happens to the sense of identity your name gives you if you suddenly change it. As with the increasing number of transgender changes, it must surely leave at least some trace of an earlier self. Not so, it seems. There are other benefits to be gained from deliberate choice.

Inventing your own name has become a way of asserting your independence. On social media it can amount to creating a new identity for yourself, sloughing off the person born to your routine existence and adopting the looks, opinion and lifestyle of your favourite celebrity. The abundance of created names on Facebook and Twitter show just how willing people are to abandon their family name and strike out into the realms of fantasy. It's now possible to have several identities and live an imagined life in each of them. Under such disguises people conduct love affairs with strangers, play-act their way into relationships, offer the world an idealised version of themselves. These identities, shaped and named as people want them, can come to seem more real than their originals hunched over their iPads in lonely and furtive isolation. There seems a high risk of losing touch with who you originally are and where you come from. It might turn out that to feel oneself nested, however uneasily, within a community of Rowlands, or Millers, Taylors, Smiths or Joneses will offer the stability that both individuals and society need.

People with a strong sense of self and a lifetime spent displaying it – I mean artists – will continue to change names. There was a time when everyone knew who you were and where you came from. So Leonardo came from Vinci, Veronese was from Verona, and Doménikos Theotokópoulos's name proved too awkward for the Spanish who simply knew him as the Greek: El Greco. The worlds of film and pop shaped names for the sake of style and memorability from the start. By now, most of us know that Bernard Schwartz, Betty Perske, Norma Jeane Mortenson, Doris Kappelhoff, Frances Gumm, Maurice Micklewhite, Reginald

Dwight and Robert Zimmerman grew up to be Tony Curtis, Lauren Bacall, Marilyn Monroe, Doris Day, Judy Garland, Michael Caine, Elton John and Bob Dylan. In the British pop scene of the 1960s impresario Larry Parnes was set on giving his hopeful new pop idols names to help them along: today Marty Wilde, Tommy Steele, Georgie Fame, Vince Eager and Jess Conrad all have a sameness that betrays the one imagination that gave them birth. Larry Parnes himself stayed Larry Parnes.

The frenzy for new names has accelerated: once David Bowie called his son Zowie Bowie, the cat was out of the bag. Names were the playthings of parents, and when the amusement palls the afflicted children are free, it is hoped, to change without suffering any loss of identity. (Zowie Bowie became Duncan Jones, and a successful film director.) Celebrities now name their children Gulliver, Bear, Romeo, Karma, presumably in the knowledge that if they don't like them when they're older they'll change . . . possibly to Colin, Graham or Nigel . . . names that by then will sound exotic and strange.

Meanwhile, somewhere a stand is being made. Sober countries such as Iceland, Denmark and New Zealand are laying down the law, the law of which names are acceptable. Iceland has a national register of names it approves of: a mere 1800 female and 1700 male. Anything else needs official permission The ruling is meant to help preserve the Icelandic language: approved names must conjugate in Icelandic. In a population of a third of a million, there must be a high chance of meeting yourself on the high street, the plots of novels could prove confusing (it was Aron who did it. Eh?). Denmark too has an approved list, but nothing beats the stand made by New Zealand. A couple there named their daughter Talula Does the Hula From Hawaii; the child was so embarrassed she would later tell her schoolfriends she was called K. The case came to law in 2008 and the judge ruled the child was at the risk of ridicule. There is no record of what name she was subsequently given: perhaps Joan . . . nice and safe. Grrr.

———

Somewhere in a Suffolk garden is a stone. It was put there by me in 1998.

I had taken some time to find the right size and shape. I would describe its size exactly to you but for the fact the garden is no longer mine. Nor is the stone.

But it was and remains a two-foot cube of rough-hewn granite. I went to a mason's yard in Bury St Edmunds to explain what I wanted. They were bemused, but it was a sale, after all, so they didn't quibble. They understood that some-one would come and inscribe a name on the flattest, most even surface. I was, in those days, a regular attender at open days of the Suffolk Craft Society: they held displays at Aldeburgh to coincide with the annual music festival there. On one or two occasions I had commissioned pieces of work from exhib-itors: a carpet maker designed a rug for my London home, and a bookbinder had repaired and re-covered a collapsing eighteenth-century volume of law. This was more personal.

The name to be inscribed was Susan. There would be no other words on the stone, no dates, no identification. Simply Susan. And it would sit in my garden. My sister had died on New Year's Eve 1996 and been buried near her home in Hale, near Manchester. So this was no tombstone or direct memo-rial. For me it was more than that.

My sister Susan was born six years after me; my mother had

miscarried a son in the years between us. It happened after the family was involved in a minor road accident and no one made any fuss about it. I didn't know at the time, of course. What could they tell a child of four? Susan inherited the burden of being the second child. I had been the spearheading firstborn, the burden of all hopes; she was simply expected to keep up with my giddy pace. Of course she refused. Being every bit as strong-minded as me she didn't see any reason why she should follow exactly where I led. Instead she refused to take the academic path, qualified as a nurse and took on roles – most dedicatedly caring for dying children – to which I could never have aspired.

Being the younger she was still living at home when my mother's unidentified depressions held the family in thrall.

With Susan, my younger sister

Susan's life was one of what would today be called psychological abuse: threatened, emotionally blackmailed, blamed for everything that went wrong, she learned to dodge and weave her way through a daily life of misery. In family photographs of the time she is never smiling.

Finally she got away: became a student nurse at Ancoats Hospital, lived in the nurses' hostel and created a circle of friends of her own. She married a headmaster and had three children, including twins. Her death at the age of fifty-seven came as no surprise to her. At the start of that year she had remarked, 'Mother died at fifty-seven, you know . . . ' And later, 'If I make the year out . . . ' She was within months of the five years' supposed safety span from an earlier episode of breast cancer.

Now, uniquely, a stone would bear her name and nothing more. The stone engraver offered me several cursive versions of the name; I chose the simplest, which etched the five letters in cool looping shapes set at the centre of the stone surface. Then I had to decide what to do with it, where to place it, how to treat it. I had until then only been concerned that Susan's name would continue. But every object in the world has a setting, even if it is simply no setting. I now had to decide where to put it, what indeed it was for.

In the event I asked the garden designer Frankie Shrapnel to create a small plot of flowers and gravel paths that would have the stone at its centre. As it was the height of a low table we began to use it as such, setting out chairs and bringing cool drinks, where after a hot day we could watch the sun set over the horizon. We set the drinks, the bottles, the nibbles on Susan's stone.

I realised slowly that I wanted Susan to continue to have

a place in my life. We had been for some thirty years sympathetically close without ever seeing each other very often. She would certainly phone me at major crises in her life: as when she was diagnosed with breast cancer. Only when her illness returned did I become a regular visitor. Together we looked over old sepia photographs of our shared childhood, labelling for future generations those of obscure aunts and remote cousins. But mostly there were lots of pictures of the two of us, in sandals and shorts, in swimsuits on Blackpool beach, in gymslips in our scrubby back garden. And it is this Susan whose name is on the stone.

It is a half-acre garden fenced off from the surrounding rolling acres of a National Trust property. There are fine wide views in every direction, and beside the house a small dense patch of woodland netted with ivy and the pollarded growth of untidy trees. My idea was that the stone will survive us all.

I would depart this spot, new people would come, and new people after them. Chances were that they, someone, would dump the stone out of the way of their gardening plans – I imagined neat beds of coloured flowers – and most probably hump it over the fence into the woodland or the pasture beyond. Stone doesn't disappear; it doesn't degrade or erode. It stays. I fancied someone generations hence pausing long enough to decipher the strange lettering, neutral, unexplained. I even imagined archaeologists studying here – a wartime gun emplacement near by has been entirely engulfed by shrubs – scratching their heads at the enigmatic inscription. But the stone would remain. And so would the name: Susan.

No one has yet called themselves Dandelion.

Susan's stone: as it was, and as it is

On Shame

The morning is misty, with the mist lying over the path and the gardens. I walk towards the river past where the dandelions have been; now only green greets the eye. The mist hangs low over the river, which is khaki and moving slowly, without ripples. Across it, on the far bank, the meadow is shrouded in pale grey light – the sun will be coming through in an hour or two. But in this moment a shape emerges from the mist – a horse. It covers the grass with measured steps, an even pace, without purpose, intent. It moves towards the bank and then stops almost in surprise when it sees me. We look at each other across the water. It is wearing a rug; I have a parka: we are both shrouded against the chill of the morning. Then he ambles off. I am left with the mist starting to rise.

—

I was five years old and in my first year at school. There was no such thing as nursery in my day so I went from being full time in the shadow of my mother's presence to the full tilt day-long classroom experience. It was a formidable jump and my mind was leaping and racing to get things right, to belong, to be liked, to be approved of. So I was riding for a fall.

We would close our morning lessons with prayers, then disperse to our nearby homes for dinner before returning in the afternoon. This was the north, where dinner happens at midday and high tea at six. There were no school dinners at this modest Church of England establishment. But then, whose mother would not want her child home for familiar cooking and a sense of belonging? As the prayers were about to begin I put up my hand to attract the teacher's attention. 'Please, Miss, may I cross the yard?' This was how we referred to going to the lavatory. It was literally exact: two sets of little people's loos were situated in blockhouses across the tarmacked playground and going there often meant running the gauntlet of teeming rain. There was nothing particularly strange about this: plenty of homes still had outside loos. Only the newest and indeed the poshest had them indoors.

The pressure on my five-year-old bladder was great. 'No, you can wait. You should have gone at break-time.' I knew there was no appeal, and put my hands dutifully together to pray while at the same time clenching my legs together like some coy Mabel Lucie Atwell drawing. It was no good: as I bent my head down to address the Lord I saw a cascade of yellow fluid pour down my legs and puddle abundantly over my black patent shoes and neat white socks. I kept my head low, not out of piety but out of shame.

The class dispersed for dinner, the teacher pausing to rebuke me and offer no comfort. I was surrounded by titters. I walked home on my own; no one wanted to walk with me. Once at home I made no move to change my clothes, not knowing how to keep my shame to myself. I kept my secret throughout my dinner, possibly seeming rather subdued to my mother, who I regarded as the arch-judge of all behaviours and the arch-punisher of all failings. Only when she stooped to give me a hug was the truth revealed. 'What's this? What's this?' I burst into tears.

This sorry tale takes its power from the fact that, seventy-five years later, I can still see within my lowered gaze the scuffed planking of the classroom floor, the wooden struts of the desk at which I sat, my neat and tidy feet placed correctly together, and then I can hear the Niagara roar of my discharged pee. I can even conjure up that sweet release when the bladder can no longer hold and matters of discretion, taste and polite behaviour are beyond control. Shame had seized me and never let me go.

Shame is a powerful force: less than guilt but beyond embarrassment, it grips us at vulnerable moments, marking our card for the rest of our lives. Telling the tale years later over drinks with familiar friends scarcely eases the inner pain, hardly diffuses the intensity of the shameful moment. Shame is also a very tender feeling; I would like to pass on an understanding of how damaging it can be. I don't want children and young people to be shamed by adults. And I don't want adults shamed to excess by peer groups, newspapers, public opinion. Terms such as 'witch-hunt', 'scapegoat' come to mind.

Shame has undergone change in my lifetime. As an internal personal humiliation it is less of the force it was; as an external expression of community feeling it has become universal and political. It is never without impact. From an aspiring lower middle class, I grew up within two aspects of accelerating social change: physical inhibitions and class.

As I learned at the age of five the body and its functions were a source of shame . . . a view that was reinforced by my family's behaviour in the most trivial matters. Glimpses of personal nudity were to be avoided at all costs. It may be that such caution resulted from the working-class practice, essential for large families in small terraced houses, of growing boys and girls sharing the same bedroom and often the same bed. It may have been a natural safeguard against personal intimacies that were known – through Church and tradition – to be wrong. My mother had grown up in such a home and was still fastidious about these matters. The business of getting the six-year-old me changed from a dress into a swimsuit via a voluminous towel on the breezy Blackpool beach was a performance worthy of a contortionist.

Popular songs seemed to us to endorse our inhibitions – 'a glimpse of stocking was something shocking' carolled the gay Cole Porter back in the 1930s. It was a lyric that quickly referenced 'the olden days'. But working-class Manchester was slow to pick up on the sexy sophistication of Manhattan, let alone Bloomsbury. We were only just getting over the trial of Oscar Wilde, so we were well behind the times. This would in its own time spark another source of shame: the shame of being out of date.

As I grew up fashion seemed to reveal more and more of the female body; in the 1970s the *Sun* newspaper took to publishing women without clothes. So there was much individual tut-tutting and exclaiming 'She ought to be ashamed . . . ' Young women of course relished the shock they were causing, lowering their necklines, raising their hems to outrage their elders and impress their peers. Today there is almost nowhere to go with the skimpiness of dress: hem and neckline are virtually converging. So the mode is now led by the most outré of pop stars. Lady Gaga – a serious performance artist – once draped herself in slices of raw meat. For some reason it didn't catch on.

At the same time, the private tut-tutting has turned into wider and heavier condemnation escalating into the disapproving weight of public opinion The fact of women revealing their bodies is now subject to the new Puritanism: 'she'll get what she deserves', 'she was asking for it'. The eagerness of the more censorious to condemn has become part of the debate around definitions of rape in society. Much has changed since my childhood in the 1940s, much stays the same, and shame somehow still attaches to women.

Women's bodily functions were also problematic. As long as all references were kept discreetly within the home and the circle of close woman familiars, matters of menstruation, pregnancy and childbirth could be shared. But I grew up with the distinct impression that half of the human race – the male half – knew nothing about how they came into the world. Not that I was any the wiser: I had no brothers and the nudity taboo meant I never saw the male body. I learned male anatomy from statues in the museum, and even then I had to be careful not to be seen looking. My mother always excused this prudery as being about 'private matters'. And very private they were: we only shopped for sanitary towels when there could be seen to be no men in the shop; the goods were, of course, kept below the counter. The misfortune of having a speck of blood accidentally smear a skirt was a matter of acute embarrassment. The idea of having condoms on sale, let alone on display, was beyond comprehension. Women who were pregnant wore loose, flowing garments and as far as possible stayed at home for the last month of the nine. Breastfeeding was for home.

All this was gloriously blown apart for my generation by Hollywood and its displays of nubile women and the seductive antics of Jane Russell, Brigitte Bardot and Marilyn Monroe. Earlier I had been offered the safe – though now distinctly suspicious – charms of Shirley Temple, the strapping health of the young Judy Garland. And Snow White, whose chaste and vacuous hope that 'someday my Prince will come' stood in for delayed gratification. I, in my eagerness, lapped it all up, and with it the confusion of titillation, shame and secrecy. Happily in the decades since, young Western women have grown up free and uninhibited. It is not a universal blessing.

Class, too, was where there were clever and knowing ways of extending shame. The victory of the Labour Party in 1945 shook the prevailing power hierarchy. Churchill had been an outstanding war leader, totally absorbed in the matter of winning and thus neglectful of his role as leader of the Conservative Party. Neither they nor he envisaged defeat when the war ended on 8 May. In his first campaign broadcast Churchill made the casual but toxic mistake of declaring that the introduction of socialism 'would require some sort of Gestapo'. Hayek's book *The Road to Serfdom* had been published in 1944 and it's thought he was influenced by it, just as Margaret Thatcher was to be three decades later. When the votes were counted the Labour Party had an overall majority of 183 seats.

The polls had been swinging Labour's way throughout the campaign but such was the sense of entitlement among traditional Conservatives and their supporters that the Labour win came as a shock; there were mutterings of an ungrateful nation kicking their great leader in the teeth. Nor were they prepared for what was about to arrive: a government pledged to represent the working classes, to enact the Beveridge Report of 1942 and commit itself to something called the Welfare State. I use capital letters for it now, as is often done, but at the time the phrase did not have the resonance nor the status it has earned since. Churchill for his part had privately spoken of Beveridge as 'an awful windbag and a dreamer'. No wonder they didn't see it coming.

Nonetheless, there was a growing awareness that the balance was tipping . . . that the working classes were extending their sway and that, thanks to the series of punitive inheritance tax rises throughout the 1940s many of the great estates were being broken up and their owners dispossessed. With the insouciance of entitlement much of this was turned to humour and mockery. Evelyn Waugh – an apologist for rather than himself a member of the upper classes – had already, in his novel *Put Out More Flags*, had a good deal of fun at the expense of poor East End evacuees moved to the countryside. Then in 1954 the linguist Alan S. C. Ross wrote a scholarly article on the difference that social class made to English usage: he differentiated U – upper class – from non-U – non-upper – as used, it was implied, by the newly aspiring middle class. The debate took fire, its flames fanned by Nancy Mitford in an essay, 'The English Aristocracy', published in *Encounter* in 1954. It touched a nerve . . . many nerves. The essay, along with contributions from Waugh and Betjeman, was reprinted as *Noblesse Oblige: an Enquiry into the Identifiable Characteristics of the English Aristocracy*. It set the agenda for decades of the finely calibrated class snobbery which the British seem to love. And in the mid-1950s it hit me and my generation of lower-middle-class scholarship students right where it hurt.

I had been taught the wrong language all along. My mother, who had an awesome respect for her betters, was keen that we should acquire the genteel speech and manners that set them above us. I had been sent for elocution lessons to iron out my Stockport accent and had instilled in me the correctness of speech that included serviette, settee, lounge, toilet, mirror and, when mishearing someone, Pardon? In the 1950s my life was transformed. I won a scholarship that took me from the cosy Lancashire speech of my grandparents and the would-be gentility of my mother to the awesome correctness of Cambridge University. Here I found many of my fellow students at Newnham College were from grand places such as Roedean, Cheltenham Ladies' College, Benenden, St Paul's, and with their honking voices and knowing confidence confused me even further. I seemed to be swimming against several tides at once; my answer was to swim all the harder, seeking comfort in drink whenever my meagre confidence flagged.

When all this experience was distilled in U and non-U debate I felt compelled to switch suddenly to napkin, sofa, drawing room, lavatory, looking glass and What? The last — what? — had always been pointed out to me as a child as excessively abrupt and rude. So I was confused about not only the nature of the language but the spirit behind each particular enunciation: 'What?' I was soon barking with relish at my cowering parents. Shame was the penalty for getting it wrong.

This was, of course, when received pronunciation ruled at the BBC, when Gracie Fields – a Lancashire mill girl who sang her way into the nation's heart with her rendition of 'Sally in Our Alley' – was seen as common, while Vera Lynn's 'The White Cliffs of Dover' was acceptably middle class. To be aspirational was seen as somehow dishonest, aspiring to be something you weren't. And such inauthenticity was shameful.

Shaming someone for their class is still going on, but now there is revenge in the air. The despised and rejected have risen up against their tormentors. Andrew Mitchell's career crashed over his allegedly using the word 'pleb' to describe a policeman; public abuse was heaped on David Mellor for his condescending rant against a taxi driver. Emily Thornberry's photograph of a beflagged house with a white van parked outside was declared snobbish and patronising; her career took a lurch. This is all largely possible because of the internet, without which these slurs would rest in obscurity. I am not sure that we aren't opening the floodgates here: naming and shaming has become a political weapon.

How much shame can we feel for the past? And what does that shame feel like? Certainly not like the tortured embarrassment of the child or the social isolation of the teenager. There is something else going on when people who haven't consulted us make grovelling apologies on our behalf for things that happened when we weren't alive. This is the highly political business of the collective apology. It seems to have arisen in the West as a way of confronting political issues long past but still reverberating. Global twenty-four-hour news keeps them boiling, its tone loaded with the language of blame and outrage. Journalists seek out causes: why something happened, who did it, how it can be remedied and avoided in future. Some think, leave it alone, things were different in the past, others demand apologies, redress. This is a huge agenda for civil society to take on board.

We all want wrongs to be put right, but the burden of history will only bear so much agonising. In the 1960s I knew a young American draft-dodger seeking refuge in London from the Vietnam War who committed suicide because he couldn't bear the guilt of what his country was doing to innocent Vietnamese peasants. The collective apology is a way of trying to redress the wrongs of history made on behalf of the living who can't as individuals do much about it.

———

I pause to look out of the window. Outside everything is growing into life . . . and fading. The cottage window opens onto green, branches and bursting buds and the churchyard beyond. The daffodils are past their prime now. Was there ever such a springtime for daffodils? Everywhere swathes of yellow: roadside verges dense with them; front gardens of pubs and houses shrieked with yellow – it almost burnt the eyes. It certainly lifted the spirits. Now the gaudy trumpets are muted, withering to brown and hanging their heads. It might make one sad. There is further passing: the cherry blossom has passed its peak and there are more petals on the grass than on the branches. On the magnolia only a few flowers remain; the grass is strewn with white.

But I open my window and a branch of wisteria reaches in

The cherry tree sheds its blossom

to me. Its mauve flowers are emerging from the moth-furred buds. I lean out and see others along the branch tingeing the air with faint pink mist. There is promise of great showers of mauve to come.

The spring air takes some of the solemnity from my thoughts: one day none of this will matter, will not matter at all. What matters is the beauty of the world, the succeeding seasons . . . leaf and bud, flower and birdsong.

———

Human attempts to redress past wrongs feel lumpen and late. I'm not sure when the practice began, but like many of these new traditions it only breaks through when it's been happening for some time. By now the apologies are piling up, many made by political figures who by their inclusive language seem to be rolling me up in their expressions of regret whether I have a sense of individual shame or not.

Within a month of being elected Prime Minister Tony Blair was in Ireland expressing his sorrow at the Irish Potato Famine. The occasion was a concert held in County Cork to commemorate the disaster that claimed millions of lives. Blair's letter was read to an audience of fifteen thousand. In it he declared:

> The famine was a defining event in the history of Ireland and Britain. It has left deep scars. That one million people should have died in what was then part of the richest and most powerful nation in the world is something that still causes pain as we reflect on it today. Those who governed in London at the time failed their people.

It is clear what Blair was about. In a radio interview with me in 2008 he explained that his family's background gave him a foot in both camps of the Troubles – he has family with both Protestant and Catholic backgrounds. This gave him the sympathy and the language to speak to each side from within its own argument. And he was able to use this empathy in private conversation as he moved the country to what is perhaps his largely unacknowledged achievement, the Good Friday Agreement in 1998.

It was twelve years later that Prime Minister David Cameron stood at the dispatch box of the House of Commons and apologised for the actions of British troops on Bloody Sunday, the day in 1972 when soldiers opened fire on unarmed civil rights campaigners, killing fourteen of them:

I know that some people wonder whether nearly forty years on from an event, [if] a Prime Minister needs to issue an apology. For someone of my generation, Bloody Sunday and the early 1970s are something we feel we have learnt about rather than lived through. But what happened should never, ever have happened . . . The government is ultimately responsible for the conduct of the armed forces and for that, on behalf of the government, on behalf of our country, I am deeply sorry.

His statement was made on the day the Saville Report was published, following an inquiry that had lasted twelve years and cost some £200 million. It had been instituted by Tony Blair in 1998 during talks with Sinn Fein that would lead to the Good Friday Agreement.

It has largely been heads of state and government leaders making these apologies while in office. In 1995 President Chirac apologised for France's role in the persecution of the Jews in the Second World War; in 1997 President Clinton apologised to African American men who had been used in medical research – the Tuskegee syphilis experiment – without their knowledge or agreement; in 2008 Kevin Rudd apologised to Australia's indigenous peoples for the forced separation of the Torres Strait children from their families over a large part of the twentieth century; in the same year the Canadian Prime Minister Stephen Harper apologised for the Indian Residential School system in which 150,000 aboriginal children were taken into 132 schools throughout Canada. In 1988 President Reagan apologised to more than eighty-two thousand Japanese Americans for their internment during the Second World War, awarding compensation of some $1.6 billion to them and their heirs. The thought occurs that if the USA were to apologise for slavery it would bankrupt the nation.

Above all, it is the Papacy that has made the most extensive apologia. Given that a substantial part of its remit is cherishing and sustaining the consciences of its 1.2 billion members world-wide, and that throughout much of its history the theory of its own infallibility has been central to its regime, there was a good deal of surprise at the scale of John Paul II's expressed regrets. They covered substantial parts of the history of Western Europe: the trial of Galileo; the execution of the Catholic priest/reformer Jan Hus; the brutal conquest of Latin America by the Spanish; the Crusades and the attack on Constantinople; the tortures of the Inquisition; the violation of ethnic rights; the treatment of gypsies and Cathars; and the failure to con-demn the Holocaust. More recently, sexual abuse scandals have shamed the Catholic Church into further apologies.

I don't know when I first became aware of Muslim people and their different culture. Growing up in a country with a primarily white population and still riding the tide of imperial superiority, Islam was a far-away concept in books and paint-ings. I knew from the fascination of nineteenth-century artists such as Delacroix that the East was an exotic land. Certainly Muslims seemed exotic, strange, rare, with their own rules and behaviour in which I took little interest. Gradually this changed, and by the 1970s multiculturalism dominated public attitudes, encouraging us all to celebrate and respect different cultural groups. For those of us who'd grown up in a largely white, Christian Britain this called for more awareness of how we should speak: it was sometimes hard, suppressing the habits of a lifetime. As late as the 1980s I asked a dark-skinned BBC producer where he came from; there was a good deal of huffing and puffing as I was bundled by my editor into her office and told it was offensive to ask such a question. Why? I am genuinely interested. The answer, it transpired, was that his parents came from Sri Lanka, but he had been born in Streatham. Right; I now lived in a new world order in which it was possible to cause offence with what I had thought was an innocent query. Language itself was becoming embroiled in shame and disapproval.

It is harder for older people to keep up with the new modes; it is of course quite correct that we do so. Indeed it is imperative. The old language stereotypes endorse outdated political values and judgements. When I was young golli-wogs were popular presents and *The Black and White Minstrel Show* got massive television audiences. All this had to go. But nothing stays the same for ever: I am shocked by the way rappers refer to women as bitches. What is even stranger is how all this linguistic evolution has been increasingly caught up in the legislation of the country as we struggle to control how people speak. Words themselves can now constitute chargeable offences: hate crime, stalking and trolling. Calling someone a pleb can threaten someone's political career. So can referring to the people of bongo-bongo land. Apologies and shame follow.

There is a new kind of shame that's arrived here in my lifetime. When I was younger it existed out of Western sight and awareness. But it is now within our society, affecting people who carry British passports and have been through the ceremonies that now create British citizens. It is the shame that families claim to feel when their daughters break the cultural code and make their own choice of partner and of life: at the extreme, it leads to so-called honour killings. Such crimes make shocking headlines, and quite rightly. Parents have gone to jail in Britain for killing daughters who refused either to accept the marriage arranged for them or to reject Western friends and mores. What's more, they have often been unrepentant, insisting that it is part of their cultural identity to sustain traditions.

I had a bewildering experience of this at first hand. I was sitting in the holding pen of an airport, the point at which passengers gather before filing onto the plane. I was approached by a young woman – in her late teens or early twenties. She was quite dazzling. Asian in appearance, she was very elaborately dressed in a brightly coloured salwar kameez and decked with an abundance of jewellery that gave off a gentle tinkling sound when she moved. She approached me very discreetly, minimising her movements and keeping her voice low. But she was desperate. 'Can you help me please, I don't know what to do.' She was being taken by her family back to Pakistan where she was to marry the man they had chosen. She had indeed left it late to protest.

I was totally bemused by her approach. I knew nothing about her, about her family, about her faith, their background, nothing. I was at once shocked, thrown into sudden tension about what to do. I felt I should do something; I must do something. Yet the very helplessness of the situation was obvious, if not laughable. What could anyone possibly do? This was a last-minute bid with no space or time to spare: it was like one of those last-minute sequences in a thriller movie where people are running across concourses, fleeing towards flights, making a glamorous dash to snatch success from the jaws of catastrophe. But that only happens in movies.

The sudden tension made it hard to think. I wished I hadn't been the one she had chosen to speak to. I asked her what she wanted: 'Not to go, not to go.' People were filing in, in their drab Western clothes, their blank faces focused on newspapers or books. I knew they were deliberately not catching my eye. And here was this bright explosion of beauty and grace tugging at my arm. I did the only thing it occurred to me to do: I went to speak to the uniformed airline officer taking the tickets and making final checks. I explained that someone was being made to travel against their will. I indicated the girl – it wasn't diffi- cult. Although slightly built she stood out, bright and gorgeous among the rest of the travellers. The airline officer took it in her stride. 'Right, thank you.' Her face registered no expression of any kind. I had done all I could; I stood there helplessly. The young girl was watching and saw what I had done.

The tannoy called out seat numbers. I fumbled with my ticket. And nudged my way along in the queue. So that was it then. Story over. Throughout my flight my mind was dragged back time and again to wondering what the outcome had been. I would never know. The episode left me excited by the drama of it all but also confused by my response – could I have done more, what options did I have . . . and angry to think that a family would go to such lengths to impose its will. What tiny corner of this alien culture had been revealed to me?

On Looking

I am in the cottage near the river. I walk in the church-yard and examine tombstones. As in many other parishes, most of the horizontal memorials have been moved leaving only a scattering of headstones. This has been done to make grass-cutting easier. It is practical and efficient, but it changes the traditional disposition of the crowded throng we once knew, making it more like a wide green garden. Here the grass is thick and mossy, bumpy with uneven ground – presumably where the coffins lie below. It feels somehow safe, even cosy in the warm sunlight. A restful place for old bones, scarcely identifiable one from the other.

—

What is my first visual memory? I would like it to be something grand and significant, laden with the promise of the future, freighted with the significance of the times. It is nothing like that: for some reason, in my mind's eye I see the surface of a door – it is of varnished brown wood with a curling cut-out motif fixed at eye height. I am seeing at eye height because I am being held in my father's arms, or more probably as a small toddler humped onto his hip as he pushes the door open. The image is not in any way memorable but it has survived eighty years of looking and seeing. So it is clearly not anything to do with aesthetics – my first view of the Derbyshire hills, for example. That would come later. It is nothing to do with powerful events: the bombing of Manchester lit up a glow in the sky we could see some ten miles to the south. I was taken into the garden and was lifted up, again by my father, who was pointing out what to look at as a witness, as he saw it, to historical events.

The varnished wooden door was ajar and I was being shown my new home. We moved into the pebbledash mock-Tudor semi in about 1936: so the fact the image has lived with me was probably to do with my sense of my parents' excitement at the occasion, together with my father's loving attention, of which I was to have a great deal in my life. As we settled into this new house – brown moquette furniture was soon crowding the rooms – pictures began to go up on the walls. Again I was lifted by my father to look at them and to have their stories explained. My parents' choice was governed by what was available as much as by taste, and that, in the 1930s world of lower-middle-class families, would not have been much. Over the mantelpiece hung a reproduction of Frederic Leighton's *Captive Andromache* – in reality a gigantic canvas thirteen feet long, reduced to humble dimensions of some eighteen inches. The captive Andromache, shrouded in black, stands isolated among surrounding women who are engulfed in swirling coloured garments. But the reason my father would lift me up was because on the lower right-hand side was a family group: the mother held on her knee a small baby, who was reaching out and squeezing its father's nose. That was, for me, the point of the painting. I would insist on being lifted to see this family that so mirrored my own, and I in turn would squeeze my father's nose. Of such repetitive childhood treats are lifelong bonds created.

In these early memories I am constantly in my father's arms. Where is my mother? She is of course the busy house-wife, constantly cleaning and washing, dusting and polishing, shopping and cooking, washing dishes and ironing clothes. Her aim is to have the perfect house, and having a child around threatens that perfection.

It is my father who is the more indulgent, lifting me, swinging me round, even bathing me at a time when it was considered odd for a father to do such things. I remember the song we sang together as I played with a toy boat. 'A little ship was on the sea, it was a pretty sight, / It sailed along so prettily, and all was calm and bright.' The refrain fixed the last phrase – 'all was calm and bright' – in my mind and it became a family response when asked how things were: all was calm and bright. It is just the sort of phrase I shall sing if I develop dementia and, as many do, revert to the songs of childhood. And there will be no one to know what it signifies.

It signifies my father, whose closeness to his children was exceptional. I would grow up confiding in him my hopes and fears, sharing the excitement of my schooldays, the loves and loss of teenage angst. In my junior years he sat in a chair close by while I did my homework, reading a book, never interfer-ing, just being there in case he was needed. On one occasion my art homework required me to draw a bird. I drew an owl – in pencil. The teacher was impressed; too impressed.

'This can't be your own work, someone else must have done this.' I replied, as my father had told me to: 'No, I drew it all myself, but my father made me rub it out until I got it right.'

Looking back now at the dynamics of the family, I can see that my bond with my father may have tipped the balance away from my mother, both for myself and even for him. They had met and been colleagues at work, shared the great Argentinian adventure, spoke Spanish when they wanted to shield their conversations from me, discussed details of my father's work. She was, he told me, far brighter than he was. She had studied engineering and understood all about his projects. But then, as was expected in those days, she moved into the world of domestic concerns. She addressed them with as much commitment as everything else: striving for perfection and resenting the endless routines that come with housework. The fact was neither my father nor her children were interested in that world. We took it for granted. We only noticed if it failed to run smoothly, which was rare. Otherwise we took her for granted too. She began to fall into depressive silences. When I started to do well at school and university became a possibility, I think she was jealous. But we never spoke of these things. We didn't have the words; people didn't talk of their feelings. She became bad tempered; 'difficult', we called it. To confound the situation, my father confided in me: what could be done, how could we cope? It's easy enough with hindsight and the whole panoply of therapeutic talk and analysis to see what was happening. As a lived experience, back then, it was hurtful and unhappy.

My father had always wanted to be an artist. At Chetham's, his talent had been noted but he was the eldest son and expected to learn a trade, to ensure a steady income. It would be his younger brother Arthur who became the artist. Perhaps it was my father's eye for art that schooled my own. As I grew I learned that there were many more paintings like the *Captive Andromache* in the nearby metropolis of Manchester. I would do lots more looking and seeing in its art gallery in my growing years. Its fine collection of pre-Raphaelite paintings seeded a love of glamorised historical paintings and a fondness for the sentimental anecdote in paint. Such fondness has never left me.

I am speaking of art history, in which I was to have steady guidance at my grammar school. But the habit of looking applied to the world at large. My eye was engaged by the meadows of flowers that surrounded me as I grew up. When I came to read and learn about D. H. Lawrence I noticed that I shared with him the experience of growing up in surroundings that gave me access to both town and country: better than that, it melded the two at the fringes of industrial life so that the senses nurtured by one infused the other. My home was on an unmade road that petered out into fields within fifty yards of our front gate. Lawrence's house was the last in a terrace of miners' cottages that gave on to fields and farmland beyond. He writes beautifully of this situation, describing, in *Sons and Lovers*, the nearby farm and the rutted paths and hedgerows that took him there. This juxtaposition of the sprawling town and the unbridled countryside is one of the happiest to grow up in. It brought me the delight of trams, and the love of wild grasses and flowers.

———

In the here and now, in the lanes and by the river, the air is full of birdsong. I try to track it but my eye isn't quick enough.

A bush in leaf appears to be full of linnets. They chatter and flutter. I see a lonely blackbird on a branch, his yellow beak opening to give out perfect sound. Down from the cottage and sitting by the river I am startled by the sudden swirl of wings as two Canada geese – large and clumsy – land on the water. They look around, clearly don't feel it's for them, and with another swirl of wings take off over the budding candles of the horse chestnut tree. I like being part of this humming life: small incidents all around me, an anthology of spring in full force. Time to be at my desk. I go inside almost unwillingly, leaving the seasons to progress without me.

———

I must have been about four when I was allowed out to wander 'no further than the field'. To me it seemed a vast prairie: a small mound over in the corner was known by us children as Everest. I remember wading breast-high through the waving grasses, and seeing the insects running up and down their stems; I would sit and look. I would tickle them with another grass, teasing them to run away. Lower down, I crouched where the vegetation was more dense and full of rustling and lurking things; I would sit on my haunches, watching their coming and going. I knew nothing about them but was simply content to sit there, out of sight of the adult world, just being, knowing nothing of purpose or intent. As I grew older I began to know their names. I began to pick and press samples of the flowers (was I collecting for a Brownie badge, I wonder) treating them as trophies for my collection. I would look details up in the *Observer's Book of British Wild Flowers* – one in a series of small reference books, which I acquired one by one as rewards for minor successes. I still have some of the flowers – over fifty varieties – I collected and pressed between large and now curled pages. But what I remember most fondly is the free unquestioning spirit of the child.

The world was all around me, but the abundance of created images with which we are surrounded today was unimaginable to us. There was a shortage of paper in wartime so newspapers were thin affairs, magazines with pictures thought of as something special. My parents had a *Pears Cyclopaedia* and a set of *Everyman's Enyclopaedia*, kept in the chilly front room in a bookcase with glass frontage: looking things up was regarded as a momentous event brought on by a homework impasse or, as far as my parents were concerned, a squabble about a crossword clue. Looking required almost formal effort and the knack of making the most of few resources. My grandparents had a huge family Bible where all family events were recorded in my grandfather's copperplate handwriting. It had interleaved within its pages reproductions of apocalyptic biblical scenes in the style of John Martin: here was the flood and the ark, the slaying of Goliath, Samson bringing down the temple, the exodus from Egypt. I positively gloated over the richness of the imagery. As the adults sat chatting my granny knew what would keep me quiet. And the images stayed with me.

Wartime brought a fantastic thirst for news and images. We regularly tuned in to hear the radio bulletins of battles raging. I remember most vividly the battle for Caen that lasted from 6 June to 9 July 1944. The D-Day landings had stalled and there was fighting and massive slaughter throughout the city. We depended on words not images. The television service had closed for the duration of the war. But the words were exciting enough. A whole generation of BBC reporters with outstanding expressive skills used evocative and even poetic language to conjure up what they were seeing for their listeners. People such as John Snagge, Frank Gillard and Richard Dimbleby made the language sing with their fluency . . . their slips and errors of judgement too. Alvar Lidell introduced the report of El Alamein with: 'I'm going to read you the news, and there's some cracking good news coming . . . ' Wartime didn't require anyone to be unbiased. And we hung on their words day after day.

If we wanted images of war we went to the cinema, where newsreel reports would catch up with what had happened days before. The newsreels were in black and white and jubilantly patriotic: in the teeth of disasters they remained buoyantly optimistic. I never knew that our side was doing anything but winning; there were just occasional hold-ups along the way – Dunkirk, Dieppe, Arnhem.

And then there was *Picture Post*, founded in 1938. Within a decade photojournalism had become part of our lives. We had known of the *Illustrated London News*, which since 1842 had been telling the world of news events with engraved photographs: Roger Fenton, notably, had brought back pictures from the Crimean War. But such a publication didn't reach where I was looking. *Picture Post* did: its sales during the war touched two million copies a week. A new world of imagery from around the world, with an upbeat, liberal editorial tone, was just what we needed. I learned from *Picture Post*, and for the first time, of the variety and strangeness of the world: I saw people in exotic clothes in distant lands leading lives that were strange to me. And I believed they would stay that way. I never imagined – there was no evidence – that these worlds would converge and become part of my own, the exotic clothes passing me on London pavements, the strange lives bringing their challenge to what some would call British values and the British way of life.

Picture Post challenged our insularity, our parochialism. Its photographs offered at a glance an expanding education far beyond the tales of triumph and empire that were what we knew. Images were beginning their steady march towards the forefront of our sensibility. More was to follow: a trickle becoming a cascade, until today our brains handle a torrent of images coming at us ceaselessly and from every direction, and at every hour. No wonder there is a boom in people seeking out religious-led retreats, hoping to recover silence and serenity.

In the 1930s I went with my parents to Argentina. And my father took a camera – a Zeiss Ikon. The idea was to keep a record of what was for us an exceptional voyage. I have the camera still: opening the heavy leather case closed with a lock and key, the stitching falls apart from age. On the camera itself a button sprang the contraption open and unfolded a pleated leather interior with moveable viewfinder and all the focusing capacity on the front. It weighs just over a pound. I no longer have the long leather tube with its button that clicked to take the photograph; it had to be unscrewed and packed away. This cumbersome object took a spool of film which was, by our standards, costly and precious and to be used sparingly. In consequence, our routine as photographers was strictly cir-cumscribed. No view however worthwhile was photographed more than once. Individuals – mostly my mother and I – were photographed full length in midshot. There were no close-ups but sometimes we would get excited by the presence of friends and bunch a whole group of them together – again full-length midshot.

The pictures were later mounted, tucked with small fixtures at each corner into albums whose dark pages were interleaved with flimsy protective paper. We were in no doubt that photographs were rare and special. The albums were put away with the *Pears Cyclopaedia* behind the glass of the book-case in the cold front room. They were brought out every so often to be viewed as a family treat. Unwittingly this upset my younger sister who had not been to Argentina and was distressed to have its delights so thoughtlessly paraded before her. It was my introduction to the triumphalist photo-boasting that is such a wicked pleasure of holiday travel.

Today we each carry a camera with us in our phone and use it on impulse round the clock. It has become a routine appurtenance of daily life. Its presence renders everything from a car crash to a riot, a protest, a tsunami a global event we can all share. It is transforming photojournalism and the conduct of wars, elections and public events. It also multiplies by incalculable numbers the visual images that now drench the planet. And in an odd reversal of priorities the most popular subject is not family, friends and interesting views, but our-selves. We have turned the camera round to face ourselves. The word 'selfie' has entered the *Oxford English Dictionary*. Is this a celebration of our individuality or a desperate bid to be noticed in a tumultuous world, to leave some record, some trace among the hubbub? I don't know. But I have stood in the Louvre in Paris as hordes of tourists have pushed and elbowed their way to see not the *Mona Lisa* itself, to examine her enigmatic smile and the gloomy background landscape, but to photograph themselves, taking it in turns to stand with the portrait behind them as though to prove that they had actually been in its presence. Never did that enigmatic smile seem more ironic.

I owe a lifetime's enthusiasm for looking to the humble postcard. We take for granted things that are cheap and abundant, but for me the postcard is special.

It began at school when the art mistress Mrs Dewhurst brought in her collection of postcards of Old Master paintings. It continued when I went travelling in Italy as a student and our enthusiasm for the art was such that we would share a bowl of spaghetti for lunch to free up lire enough to buy postcards of Masaccio, Botticelli, Ghiberti, Donatello and the rest . . . we pushed our hunger to the limit to get as many postcards as possible. The hunger has long gone, but I still have the postcards.

And then there was the holiday routine: an obligation to send postcards to family and friends. The list was never short of a dozen and the selection required the matching of picture to the personality of the recipient. They in their turn would do likewise, and in offices and on kitchen walls the summer months would bring a crop of pictures from across the globe. People rarely do that any more: where's the need? They are probably texting and phoning, sending photos by mobile phone. You can, if you choose – as lovers and anxious mothers do – never be apart for any length of time. I am currently following day by day the Facebook reports of a grandson travelling in South-East Asia.

But the postcard remains in my life; the standard shoebox is the perfect storage. I can browse and dip into a chaotic medley of images. Here's a typical peek: *Black Hat* by Alex Katz, from the Turner Contemporary gallery in Margate; *The Village School* by Jan Steen from the National Gallery of Ireland; *The Concert in the Egg* by Hieronymus Bosch from the Palais des Beaux-Arts in Lille; *Silent Light* by Rose Wylie at the Jerwood Gallery in Hastings; *View Near Naples* by Francis Towne at Birmingham Museum and Art Gallery . . . and so it goes on. A lifetime's postcards doing what I always imagined they would do, bringing visual excitement to me in my old age and keeping those look-see juices running.

Their randomness demonstrates the promiscuousness of my taste. As long as I get the sensation of my optic nerve locking on and connecting to something responsive in my brain, I have the sense of being thoroughly engaged. Bad paintings are a minor joy: *Allegory of Victory* by Le Nain in the Louvre has a voluptuous winged angel standing proud with both bare feet on the stomach of a prone naked man. It is the low horizon and the wide countryside behind them that render the whole thing particularly silly.

Postcard-collecting is called deltiology, a word coined in the 1940s to identify the surge in both postcards and their fans. There are many sub divisions: seaside postcards, First World War postcards with both sad and cheery messages (the cheery ones made sad by knowing the probable fate of their writer), advertising postcards, suffragette postcards – I have one whose rhyme begins 'This is the House that Man built' set against the Houses of Parliament. Collectors haunt car boot sales and stalls such as the one under Westminster Bridge where the detritus of lives now gone have fetched up to bring unexpected joy to someone's heart. I will not be sad if my shoeboxes end up the same way.

Postcards are all very well, but there is nothing like the real thing. The serenity of the moment, the sense of letting the world, and even the surrounding crowds, fall away and just being alone with the created work. A calmness descends: my breathing changes, I give up worldly things. It is the moment I live for in my gallery-going. Then the traditional exhortation to the grammar-school girl kicks in: don't waste time, learn something. I feel the old compulsion. I am snatched from my reverie and back in the business of acquiring knowledge. I am one of those who reads the small guidebooks handed out at the entrance; I am one of those who scours the labels, noting – and then forgetting – date, origin, materials and owner. I get caught up in facts. This, of course, has its own compulsions and fascinations. Over the years I have developed a passion for the knuckles and toes in anything by Cosimo Tura, the straining buttocks in paintings by Signorelli, the dazzling fall of robes in Pontormo; I love the asparagus by Monet, the cup and saucer by Fantin-Latour; the mysterious women turning their backs in interior paintings by Vilhelm Hammershøi. Of contemporary work I am intrigued by anything wrapped by Christo and Jeanne-Claude, anything blown up by Cornelia Parker, anything annotated by the Chapman Brothers. If this reads like the culture-hungry collecting of an enthusiastic schoolgirl, so be it.

Fantin-Latour, White Cup and Saucer

Vilhelm Hammershøi, Interior, 1898

Cornelia Parker, Cold, Dark Matter:
An Exploded View

That enthusiasm has lasted in me for some seventy years and illuminates everywhere I visit.

I am hoping to pass it on when I go. The path has already been laid. By some strange alchemy my daughter grew up to take her degree at the Courtauld Institute, one of the world's foremost centres for the study of the history of art. She wrote her PhD on Classical sculpture. My son, who works in architecture, arrives in London with a shopping list of visits to everything from White Cube to the Royal Academy, the V&A to the Serpentine; we try to celebrate London's Open House Day together every year.

Of this I can be sure: when I am no longer standing beside them, having my daughter's exposition whispered in my ear, having my son's lateral thinking adding to my insights, they will continue to enjoy what they see, and in so doing they will pass the pleasure on to my grandchildren. It is a good legacy.

Detail from Cosimo Tura, Saint Dominic

On Stuff

The early plantings have come good. The fields where I watched the young farmer sowing are now green with spinach, with chard and even a stretch of coriander. In my town garden the mint and chives are flourishing in their pots, but London growing is a tougher ask. Round the cottage the abundant green takes over, its presence overriding all else. Flowers blossom and die away . . . one colour following another in the small, neat gardens. On the river a boat is taken up and down by excited boys. Abundant summer.

—

Stuff. I like the sound of the word: immediate, explosive, shading into soothing. Stuff is what it is, the flotsam of a long life lying in drifts across my home. It will have to go. But who will want it? And how will those who want it come across it? The world is full of the dross from old houses being cleared out. The point is that for the owner – for me – it isn't dross even then. It's memories made tangible.

The path was muddy and the doll was a prized possession. I had insisted on taking it with me on the walk through the fields, the path skirting the edge of the crops, where later in the year poppies would glow among the golden corn.

In summer I used to steal away and hide among the swaying grain. But now it was spring and it was important to dodge the pools of recent rainwater. Mummy was strict about not getting my shoes muddy. She had advised against taking the doll with us as we took the short cut to the little row of shops.

The doll had come from far away. Daddy had brought it back from foreign travel. It was what men did, travelling abroad and bringing back special presents. The doll was a grown girl, not a baby. It had a waist and blonde hair cut like mine. Daddy said he had chosen it for that reason. It came from a shop called Marie-Lu; that was the name given to all the dolls they sold. They all had limbs jointed at the knees and elbow. And the head was special: it was made of porcelain and had lips and cheeks painted bright red. The eyelids blinked up and down. They clicked lightly as they did so. Under the hair on the back of the neck the word 'Germany' was embossed in the supposed pink flesh. This was odd because Daddy had not been visiting Germany; he wouldn't have wanted to. There was a war there and things that made people serious and sad.

The doll had grown-up clothes: a white petticoat that fitted her shape and was trimmed with lace. Over it a silk dress with trimmings of white braid and a sash to tie at the back. Then a bright red coat with tiny buttons and a little stitched belt, and a brown velvet collar. The doll's fingers were spread as though she were about to play the piano, and she had small lace gloves that fitted close over the splayed fingers.

I held her to me, wrapped around with both arms. There

was no hand free to slip into my mother's. 'Well, you'd better watch out: the path can be slippy.'

I heard the sound clearly enough, the sound of adults telling you what to do. But I whispered to the doll, consoling, comforting, the way you did to those in your care.

The path rose steeply, coming from behind the houses and curving upwards to join the main road. At some time builders had laid planks of wood like railway sleepers across the path to stop the ground shifting. And between there was loose gravel. The rain had loosened the sleepers' hold.

As I fell I thought only of the doll, to keep it safe, to protect the porcelain head, to save the lacy clothes from being spoiled. I saw the muddy ground and the splintery wooden plank coming up towards me. My grip tightened, both arms locked around the doll. No way of saving myself but I didn't care about that. I didn't feel the pain in my hands at first. Mostly I was aware of Mummy shouting, helping me up and shaking my shoulder. 'I told you! I told you!' I could see the back of my hands were bleeding, there was blood dripping onto my coat. But I felt no pain. This is what it is to care, I thought. This is what you must do for those you love. Mummy was now fussing about the graze to my skin and the gravelly mud embedded there. In coming days it would be painted with a painful cream recommended by the doctor. Hold on, hold on tight, I whispered to myself, clinging to my sister's arm as the cruel cream bit into the wound. Remember Marie-Lu is safe. The doll sat opposite on the chest of drawers, her bland pink face expressionless, unscathed. The agony of the cream subsided. The wound would heal.

It felt every bit as melodramatic as that: the struggle and

sacrifice to protect and rescue a frail and dependent child. How odd it was that this doll shaped and dressed like a full-scale adult gave me the sense of caring for a baby. Was it something to do with its special nature, from far away, a gift from an adored parent? The fact is I have her still: seventy-five years she has been with me, both of us moving from a world long forgotten, keeping alive in me feelings and fondnesses for people and events no one else can share. She is broken now, her detached head cradled among the discarded clothes, the articulated limbs wrenched awkwardly to fit the space of the old shoebox. When I go and they clear out the cupboards will she be tossed in some street-side skip beside stained strips of carpet and old Doc Martens? Or will she by a crazy juncture of probabilities find her way into the hands of some installation artist who will meld her into fantastic creations and go on to win the Turner Prize? Which to prefer?

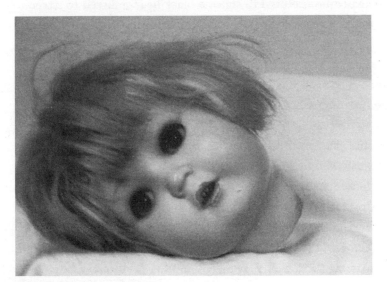

Marie-Lu, the doll from Buenos Aires

The bonfire of the teddy bears

Of course I have a teddy bear, though I don't like it much. It was given to me by a doting swain when cuddly animals were shorthand for sexual advances. I tucked it in a drawer long ago. I recently found it there: it is handsome as these things go: soft golden fur, red leather soles to his feet, a pert little nose nothing like the long snout of the natural beast. But then it is part of the panoply of toys that resemble merely themselves and not their progenitors. Think only of golliwogs. And yes, I had one of those too.

I am not fond of teddy bears and the culture of smug well-being that surrounds them. It is well established that the name and the toy itself originated at the start of the twentieth century when President Theodore Roosevelt out on a hunting expedition refused to shoot a black bear tethered to a tree to make it a no-contest target. The event was cartooned, and this inspired a toy which became a national craze as these things do. But the craze refused to die. It clearly answered a need.

The need was felt, among others, by young boys sent off to boarding school and mercilessly exposed at a vulnerable age to the teases, bullying and other interferences of fellow pupils and teachers. Their need for a comfort blanket was easily answered by the soft toys of their babyhood. John Betjeman is said to have taken his bear Archibald Ormsby-Gore up to Oxford and later died with him in his arms. The bear's arrival in Oxford came to the attention of the bright young things there, whose company Betjeman assiduously courted. Among them Evelyn Waugh – another prep-school boy – who created another teddy bear, this time called Aloysius and the perpetual friend of Sebastian Flyte in *Brideshead Revisited*. All this is very coy; as I was never a prep-school boarder shedding hidden tears into my pillow I find the whole confection rather arch.

Winnie-the-Pooh is a different matter . . . almost. It stems from a similar class background to that of the Archibald/Aloysius clan. A. A. Milne was the son of the headmaster of a small private school, and, after service in the First World War, became the author of many plays – scarcely remembered – and five slim volumes of childhood verse and tales which were and remain universally adored. They celebrate the childhood of his own son Christopher Robin and his toys, Winnie-the-Pooh, Piglet, Eeyore, Owl, Rabbit and, later, Kanga, Roo and Tigger. Milne had been a regular contributor to *Punch* and his style of gentle humour is suitably engaging. But the books' success owes much to another *Punch* contributor, the illustrator E. H. Shepard. Together they created a world of childhood innocence set in the Hundred Acre Wood destined to appeal to parents and children alike. Unhappily for the eponymous Christopher Robin, he was destined to be teased mercilessly at both his prep school and later his public school, Stowe, for the rhymes bearing his name.

None of which detracts from the popularity of Pooh – declared by *Forbes* magazine in 2002 as the most valuable fictional character of all time. Following the Disney versions the merchandising sales topped $5.9 billion. Quite good, as he might well say, for 'a bear of very little brain'. Yes, I am indeed familiar with the texts of the stories, and even indulged as a student in late-night readings aloud. The characters clearly had appeal for the soft heart of my generation: gentle humour with loveable character types. Alan Bennett – rather an Owl, I think – catches it in his broadcasts and recordings. In my days on *Newsnight* Jeremy Paxman was known as Eeyore. I still have on my shelves copies of *Now We are Six* and *When We Were Very Young* – and even a volume entitled *Winnie Ille Pu*, the Latin version. Of course, when the time comes they will all be stuff.

Books

Of all the stuff that will survive me, my shelfloads of books are the most extensive, most intractable, most problematic. Who now wants miles of books accumulated over a lifetime and representing a gallimaufry of different interests, levels of taste and degrees of usefulness?

Here are the first-edition paperbacks of all Elizabeth David's 1950s breakthrough recipes, stained with blotches of fat, pages gummy with spills, the whole yellowing mess reminding me of my own favourites. Elizabeth David's books have all been reprinted, so my ghost will not mourn their being tossed into the skip. But there is another more particular accumulation of stuff: my own collected recipes. Since the 1950s, when Robert Carrier dominated the cookery pages of *Vogue*, I have been cutting out recipes from magazines and newspapers. The habit persists to this day, a motley collection of my own particular tastes – a liking for scallops, aubergine, avocados – cut out, categorised, slipped into plastic sleeves and held within their own folder. Who would care to inherit this? I would have thought no one, until recently I had a text from my daughter: 'please send recipe for stuffed marrow'.

Yet more books

There are plenty of books that have significance within my family history but none in the outside world. It was the custom for many generations of schoolchildren to receive prizes for good work. My father earned two such, memorably inscribed. The first, awarded by Egerton Infants' School in 1908, is *Lazy John: The Boy who Would Not Work*, a large Edwardian picture book showing a bad boy getting into trouble and being redeemed by virtue. My father's Aunt Sarah, his guardian after his parents' death, was furious at the school's lack of tact. I can imagine her rounded Welsh body swelling in rage to her full five feet in height at the insult implied by the title. Whether she descended, wielding her black umbrella on the thoughtless authorities, I do not know, but she certainly made a song and dance about it and was still doing so in my day, outraged on my father's behalf although he was by then in his thirties. His other prize was more appropriate and much enjoyed by me in my teens: a copy of Charles Kingsley's *Westward Ho!* with illustrations by C. E. Brock presented in Class 2 at Chetham's for proficiency in drawing. I fell hook, line and sinker for the romantic adventures of Amyas Leigh against the dastardly Spanish, and winning the love of the shy, dark-eyed Rose Salterne. I searched the drawings for detail, of armour, of ships' rigging, of lace and velvet at cuffs and stomacher.

My father grew up to marry a dark-eyed Rose of his own and I wonder whether that early fictional romance had inclined him towards the name. Certainly at the time of the Queen's coronation in 1953, when newspapers came in search of bright college students to hail as the New Elizabethans and we self-righteously dismissed the idea as crass, I, perhaps alone of all my friends, kept silently to myself a feeling that New Elizabethans had a certain appeal. Who was to know I was thinking of Amyas Leigh and Rose Salterne?

Ars longa ... but not in my case

Of all the stuff that I leave behind, what matters to me but has little appeal beyond is the collected art created by generations of my family. It takes various forms: canvases – oil and acrylic – watercolours, clay models, drawings, pottery. If my life were an Enid Blyton story I would hold an amateur art exhibition in the village hall, the vicar would open it and neighbours would gather to marvel at our gifts. That is about the scale of it.

But then it's not among my stuff because of its merit as art. It charts the artistic impulse that runs through us all and which has always won uncritical approval from the rest when anyone showed any shred of talent. All mothers know the impulse to pin a child's drawings on the kitchen noticeboard or tape them to the fridge. But what happens as they grow up and the stuff keeps coming? I have kept a plaster cast of my son's five-year-old hand which has for me a lasting poignancy, and some collages made by my gifted teenage daughter. Now that they are both in their fifties these traces of their earlier selves have, if anything, even greater appeal for me than at the time of their making: they prompt memories, recall incidents, conjure a sense of earlier relationships. What happens to sentiment – shared sentiment – when we go?

It can only be sentiment that keeps a stack of my father's not very good oil paintings in the attic. They are there because I remember his tales of the young boy who wanted so much to be an artist, who was regarded as gifted by his teachers, who was forced to earn a living as an engineer but who in middle age signed up for night classes at Stockport School of Art and in his widower years would sit daily at his easel and work away at the resistant canvas. Often he caught a likeness: his portrait of me worked from a photograph is recognisably myself, that of the friend of his later years is a fond and accomplished portrait. I will not be the one to throw them out. Someone else will have to do it.

All their lives my parents were self-improvers. Having missed out on the education their intelligence deserved, they seized the chance in their middle years to study with the Workers' Educational Association, taking classes in classical music, modern painting ('Is Picasso having us on?') and even struggling with philosophy. My mother's big success was her pottery: she had natural gifts of taste and judgement, and the physical skills of control and concentration. As a consequence, around my home are littered innumerable pots and bowls which each bear on the underside the mark 'R.R. 1950' and later. Some I group together on their own shelf like a Morandi painting. These have already come down to me as family heirlooms. But will my children want them? Will my grandchildren? How much accumulated stuff can the generations endure?

Photographs

The world must sink under an ever-growing tide of photographs. I shall be adding my own frothy, insignificant wave.

Taking a photograph is becoming a substitute for actually looking. But the universal habit of taking a photograph of an event as if to verify your own presence there gives the photograph a strange power to intercede between ourselves and the actual happening in time. It seems people would rather have a photograph than enjoy being in the actual reality of the moment. The cheapness and slickness of technology has wrought this change.

The stuff I have charts this change. On shelf after shelf I have shoeboxes of photographs: the ones from the 1940s and 1950s contain slim yellow folders sent from the developing company with black negatives tucked within one flap and the prints themselves in the one opposite. Film was expensive to buy so we were frugal with our use. My earliest pictures are in black and white, now fading to sepia, and little more than two inches by four. Here are schoolfriends being silly, babies in prams, toddlers lurching across lawns and groups of people posing together. Sometimes, as life widened out, there is a cross-Channel ferry, the Eiffel Tower, an ancient church. This was to show people back home what abroad was like.

Photography slowly began losing that purpose: on the whole, people came to know from magazines, films and television what abroad was like. But there were still places of mystery and secrets. My photographs capture something of what it was like in Moscow in the mid-1970s, huge posters of Lenin quotations and himself embalmed in the mausoleum. Interestingly, it was absolutely forbidden to take photographs of his corpse or even walk past it with your hands in your pockets. And in China in 1983, where the entire population was required to wear the blue Mao uniform, my pictures are a historical record. This was still photography as information.

The shoeboxes eventually give way to the laptop, or rather the various memory sticks and back-up arrangements that take up so much less space. Even as they do so, the number of actual photographs multiples exponentially. No event or occasion, holiday or even visit has gone unrecorded by someone in the family. And of course we all exchange, piling up what we have taken to calling 'the archive' into reams of stuff. If every family with a digital camera or a mobile phone is doing the same the sum total of recorded images must top many trillions.

Sadly they are for the most part boring: mid-close-ups of ordinary-looking people in ordinary-looking clothes doing nothing. Who would hesitate before throwing them out the moment the hearse has left the undertaker's? And yet, there is history to think of. Where would such painstaking historians as David Kynaston find the record of social habits, details of clothes and traffic to substantiate their remorseless research? Or must it all go to the tip?

Guilty secret

Searching in an old Victorian desk that is scarcely ever opened I come upon a crime from my past . . . or indeed many crimes. The desk lid is never lifted because I know the inside is full of stuff, stuff I can't be bothered with, a selection of old greetings cards inscribed with messages that once meant a lot, a clutch of letters from a lifelong friend tied with ribbon . . . and the dark secret.

Long ago I resolved to see the world and its antiquities; the decades rolled ahead in those days and I knew I had plenty of time. Slowly over the years I have made my visits – Rome, Pompeii, Athens, Delphi, Leptis Magna, Petra, Knossos, Bagan, Agra, Madurai, Varanasi. At each I marvelled and admired, gazed and learned. But I also did something else. Choosing my moment with care – that is to say, out of the sight and scrutiny of others – I would bend down and pick up from among the rubble at my feet a small piece of fabricated material. Not a pebble or a twig, but an artefact or more specifically a small part of an artefact, made by whoever lived in the place long ago. This is technically, and probably legally, called 'looting from historical sites'.

My bag of loot now rests inside my Victorian desk. I daresay someone with a Geiger counter or the stuff that measures carbon dating could give me a reading on each one and the right scholar might even hazard a guess at the origins of the pieces, which I have in my careless tourist way neglected to label.

When she discovered me doing something antisocial my mother would declare as a logical discouragement, 'Just imagine what would happen if everyone did that.' I longed to reply, 'But everyone else isn't,' but bit my lip for fear of a clip round the ear. I have become far more law-abiding as I grow older. I have even become something of a litterphobe, deploring the pile-up of junk on any Saturday night in any city centre. It is the literal proof of my mother's wisdom. The build-up of stuff in our towns and cities, the dumping of stuff on lay-bys and in fields is a social menace. It is my own problem with stuff writ large. What are we to do with it all?

I might simply creep out one night and scatter my small pieces of brick and pottery, the curving handle, the broken tile, all over Primrose Hill. Then, come the moment television's *Time Team* or its successor comes to trace the Hill's history, there will be confusion and speculation enough to make a lively programme.

Memorabilia

Just as I despair of finding a destination for my stuff when I'm gone, a new concept comes to my rescue: memorabilia. One person's reject is another person's collectible. Surely my stuff will fit the bill somehow. I know that people collect the most surprising things: I learn – from the internet – there's a man in South Wales with more than four thousand refrigerator magnets. Whatever the impulse is that makes someone a collector of such banal objects probably has little to do with the prospect of increasing value. I can see it must give a purpose and a sense of achievement to an uneventful life. To wake in the morning fired with the thrill of the chase, the hunting-down of car boot sales, the watchful eye at school fairs, the wrangling over price, the triumph of ownership, the pride in surveying the collection . . . all these must offer small daily lifts of the spirit. Unless your choice is for Rembrandts or Wedgwood pottery, you probably have the field much to yourself. Imagine the shock of arriving at a car-boot opportunity to find yourself battling a competitor for a fridge magnet of the Tower of London.

These are small preoccupations that can grow from a mild bit of fun, then into a hobby, escalating further as they grow into an obsession. There are people entirely focused on Beatles memorabilia, or Humphrey Bogart film posters, or coronation mugs. An extensive trade has grown up to meet the need.

There is a whole world out there of people like me offering their stuff to middle men who snatch it up at boot sales and house clearances and recycle it so that it becomes someone else's stuff. Round and round it goes, 1930s sheet music, cigarette cards, royal wedding tea towels, swapping and changing hands, bringing relief to those who're getting rid of it and joy to those who've acquired it: a harmless roundelay of artefacts serving no purpose but in their very transit giving pleasure at every transaction. All I need to know is how to join the ring.

I like the idea of being my own trader. I fancy setting up a trestle table outside my house and putting all the unwanted stuff there, and a notice saying 'please help yourself'. I know people do this, and I know the stuff usually gets taken. It's popular in the sort of suburbs that are friendly without being nosy. I did it myself almost by accident. I had put a small garden table and chairs, entirely rusted through and chipped of paint, out with the household rubbish. (Yes, I know they aren't meant to take it, but it's amazing what a little negotiation can do.) Before the van and its negotiators could arrive, someone had rung the doorbell to ask whether my garden furniture was genuinely discarded and if so, could they have it please. I was delighted.

Archive

This is the posh name for memorabilia that has serious significance for scholars, or even just one scholar. Writers, film-makers, creative people generally, people in public life and American presidents do it as a matter of routine, leaving behind the record of their working lives for the better understanding of those who come after. There are museums and libraries around the world building archives of the famous and celebrated, individuals who were pioneers, who initiated change, who created great works, who entertained millions. Or who simply had a name for something or other.

For some forty years I worked in British television, when new channels, new ideas and new formats were proliferating. I was in at the start of BBC 2, which brought the total of television channels the British public could watch to three. I have reported from many parts of the globe at a time when it was unusual for a woman to be fronting a programme. What remains is the detritus of decades of programmes, failed projects, letters of rejection, messages of appreciation, scripts, rewrites, voiceovers, reviews. When I came to write my autobiography in 2003 I filed all the records I had into black boxes. And there they sit. Now researchers and archivists are showing an interest. It will be another shelfload off my mind.

Or just bury it!

I've always liked the idea of a hoard. I love it when the news breaks that a farmer turning the sod has unearthed a cache of old coins, or a builder getting down among the foundations of a demolished house comes upon a bag of old gems. The very point of this is their secret antiquity: the sudden coming to light of what was never intended to have been there. Most hoards – and there have been some thirty-five major hoards uncovered in the British Isles – have been hidden by people in flight from trouble who hope when quieter times prevail to come back and dig them up. Famously Samuel Pepys, on hearing news that a great fire had broken out in London, dug a pit in his garden and buried his Parmesan cheese. In fact, the fire never reached his house; what happened to the cheese is not recorded.

So a hoard has an antiquity that stirs excitement when we see those great swathes of coins grabbed from the loamy soil. Museums love them, and they certainly draw the crowds. The British Museum alone has five major hoards: from the Mildenhall Treasure – five thousand coins – to the 8600 items of the Cuerdale Hoard from Lancashire. Just imagine the urgency and panic that went on when they were buried: who wrapped and counted them? Who was supposed to remember the spot? Perhaps they forgot and dug elsewhere, leaving the tribe ruined and the family impoverished . . . or without cheese.

The spirit of the hoard, better known as the treasure hunt, lives on. In the early 1980s, when I began reporting for the newly launched *Newsnight*, we interviewed the artist Kit Williams, who had published a book called *Masquerade* in which fifteen elaborate drawings containing a string of clues to the burial site of a secret casket containing a jewelled golden hare. It could simply have been a clever PR stunt to promote sales of his book, but we took him on trust. The more we talked with him the more we liked him and became engaged with his clever story. And it was a story that would have a long afterlife.

The book sold hundreds of thousands of copies, and because not everyone who wanted to embark on the hunt could go after it in person Kit agreed that he would also make the award available to the first mailed solution. The jewelled hare was sealed inside a casket made of clay, apparently to foil metal detectors: Kit wanted the story solved from his clever clues rather than by routine treasure hunting. The hare lay near the Catherine of Aragon cross at Ampthill Park in Bedfordshire; significant phrases were doubly disguised as acrostics and the whole thing virtually indecipherable. It was not until three years later that a Ken Thomas sent in the solution and was announced the winner.

But that wasn't the end of it. Six years later the *Sunday Times* was to accuse the winner of being a cheat. It declared that by a chain of hints and connections the disclosure of the answer had been passed to Ken Thomas, the pseudonym of someone with links to Williams. There were splutters of indignation; Williams was deeply upset and felt responsible for the mayhem. The hare itself was auctioned at Sotheby's soon after, going for £31,900 to an anonymous bidder. Years rolled by, as years do in this kind of intrigue, and in 2009 a Radio 4 programme, *The Grand Masquerade*, told the tale; later that same year the whole saga was made into a television documentary for BBC 4: *The Man Behind the Masquerade*. Kit got to see the hare again, and later still it even went on display at the V&A. Kit himself continued his great craft of designing performing clocks: examples are on display in Cheltenham and Telford.

It all goes to show what can happen to a buried secret: what layers of skill, mystification, skulduggery and genuine pleasure unfold in the years that follow. I feel seriously tempted to take at least one small but ambiguous object of my own, wrap it in silver foil, seal it in some kind of box to give it the aspect of a genuine hoard and bury it, before I go, in some deep corner of my garden. Perhaps even beside the river where I am spending my days. That will keep them guessing.

———

The sky is high and blue over the growing fields; puffs of white cloud carry no threat. In the garden, towards the river, there is a flutter of washing on a line: T-shirts and rows of socks flapping in the warm breeze that is keeping the rain away. It's rare for a townie to see washing on a line. We have spin dryers these days. Sometimes on a train journey I catch sight of a row of billowing sheets in a garden running down to the embankment. Once, Monday mornings would have seen then in every garden in the row, our mothers cursing as the smoke from the steam trains left soot on the bleached white. No more. I suppose that's an improvement. But I miss the sweet smell of the open air that would come as you culled the washing from its wooden pegs.

Washing on the line: no spin dryers then

On Then and Now

The cottage continues to be my haven: the pocket-handkerchief garden is spilling with greenery, its pots full of colour, and small patches of useful herbs by the door. I sit in the sun at the chair and table there. Other women writers have come this way, stayed here and written their pages. The charity that owns and runs it honours Virginia Woolf's claim that 'A woman must have money and a room of her own if she is to write . . . ' and provides it. The statement was made in 1928 and – though money values have changed – the thought still resonates with women today. The room in its idyllic setting gives me the space and the quiet I need. It does the same for other writers. The tombstones in the churchyard beyond the window offer their silent record of lives past. I try to find someone who reached my own age and fail.

—

Tea into coffee

We never drank coffee. I didn't know what it was until we went for a weekend to France when I was fifteen; there they drank it all the time. Not only that, but they sat at tables outside without apparently feeling the cold or having anyone steal the chairs. How odd of the French: so entirely different from us. How could anyone expect us, British, with our good sense, cups of tea and warm woollies, to ever get on with such strange people? No wonder Mrs James was upset when her son started dating a French girl. Who knew what bad habits she might introduce him to: didn't they eat garlic and, yes, drink coffee, not only on special occasions but all the time? He'd never get used to that.

Tea was the British beverage, curiously patriotic in its origins. Once the trade with China had given way to tea sourced from Assam and brought from India on tea clippers it became a mainstay of imperial trade. In my childhood it was kept loose-leafed in tea caddies and made to an accepted ritual: spooned into a warmed teapot for an initial dousing with a splash of boiling water, two minutes' infusion then the pot filled to the brim and left for a further two minutes. Now we live in a world of teabags full of inferior leftover dust and submerged in cooling water. Even worse, in some places they bring you a cup or pot of boiled water and a teabag set separately beside it. Can this be anything other than a decline in standards?

Darning – holes

The moths are back. It seems to be getting worse. Or am I getting neglectful? If insects are set to inherit the planet when humanity has destroyed itself and the larger beasts, then the moths are making a good pitch at setting up headquarters in my wardrobes and drawers. Each season – which season that is I'm never quite sure – I buy a new set of repellent equipment from the local hardware shop: small plastic pyramids that have refills of sticky poison and take up their position under sofas and behind cabinets. I have even seen them hanging behind the benches in the House of Lords. Also small white balls that give off subtle repellents inoffensive to the human nose – the olfactory equivalent of dog whistles. These get scattered throughout drawers, along with chunks of cedar wood and pretty little bags of lavender purchased on the internet. The whole defensive campaign proves very short-lived, because if I don't regularly renew the lot of them their power fades and the armies of moths sally forth from their hidden havens and attack sweaters, dresses, carpets and cushions all over again.

Is it getting worse? In my parents' time, opening their wardrobe doors was to be hit in the face by a storm of camphor scent so powerful it clung to the clothes and lingered into the outside world where my aunts and my mother would venture forth shrouded in a cloud of it. Pharmacology has clearly moved on and found less noxious treatments, but in doing so have they abandoned the killer power of the unchallenged camphor? I might need it back.

I have a hole in my sweater. It is a handsome garment of textured wools and cashmere that I am unwilling to toss out simply because of a single small hole. But there are more; indeed, looking fore and aft I find constellations of holes where moth colonies have been having a feast while my back was turned. Look! This was an expensive and attractive sweater. I am loath to throw it out. I have two options: to mend or not.

Growing up in the thrifty forties, I was co-opted from the age of ten into an activity known as the weekly darning. It was usually timed to happen on an evening when a popular programme was on the BBC Home Service, say *Monday Night at Eight*. Either my mother or I sat in an armchair nursing a basket of newly washed but holey socks. At hand lay a sewing basket full of wools of different shades and the essential tool of the darning mushroom. This gadget was plunged into the damaged sock and held firmly behind the offending hole. It was intended to make it easier to darn the hole. In fact, I rarely used it: I had honed my skills to such a fine point as not to need it and yet still deliver the repair to my mother's satisfaction.

A good darn began with the choice of an exactly matched strand of wool or cotton, not only the colour but the ply compatible with that of the sock. The darning needle, once threaded and anchored with a tiny stitch of its own, then circled the hole taking in all the ragged edges and loose-hanging stitches before gently drawing them as close together as could be achieved without bulking the surface of the sock out of shape. Then the real skill began: the passing of thread to and fro across the hole, not dragging the edges together but laying out a line of parallel threads when could then be used when the needle switched direction and wove its way in and out of the established weft. The result would look good, hold the shape of the sock and renew its wear for another few weeks. Only socks where multiple darns had built up were discarded, as such a bulky lump of discomfort made walking hard. Such darning applied only to socks, woolly and dark in winter, cotton and white in summer.

A new pair was a special treat.

I could darn my sweater. I remember how to do it. But I hesitate. People don't seem to darn any more. The modern way is to let the holes exist, to leave them open and visible as though they were part of the design. Indeed, having holes in things has entered the repertoire of fashion design. It began with Elizabeth Hurley's famous Versace safety-pin dress worn at the premiere of *Four Weddings and a Funeral* in 1994. Since then, the idea of a half-finished garment has become a signature of many styles. Fashion houses vie to have the more elaborately torn jeans. Somewhere in South-East Asia bewildered factory workers are being instructed to take perfectly good jeans and then slash them across the knee and down the shin, to patch them with flowery material that deliberately doesn't match, to stonewash them so they look as faded as if they'd survived several years roaming with the hobos on the plains of America.

Or I could throw it away. This is distinctly not to be wished. I come from the save-string-and-elastic-bands generation, brought up in wartime to cherish every scrap and morsel as part of the fight to defeat the Hun. In the post-war years we were further burdened with news that millions were starving across Europe and the people of India never knew what it was to have a decent meal. My sweater stays. I wear it casually, making no effort to conceal the defect as 1940s decorum would have had me do. Instead I feel rather smug comfort in the company of my grandchildren. I am not, surely, that cut off from their way of life. Now, perhaps, I can even nudge towards their own bewildering culture. I can at least make an attempt: look, I have holes in my sweater!

Clothes into brands

According to the Whig interpretation of history, civilisation is constantly improving and progressing, led by the enlightened thought and politics of British values. I was at Cambridge in the 1950s when Professor Butterfield's lectures were all the rage. His book *The Whig Interpretation of History*, first published in 1931, denounced this view, debunking the then prevailing notion of traditional historians – Macaulay, Trevelyan – that British history since the seventeenth century had been advancing the attributes of civilised values that led the world, and this was seen – in the style of *1066 and All That* – to make life better for all, and to be getting better all the time. Butterfield used the term Whig to express his disapproval of its simplistic assumptions. And in some arenas they still hold sway: now that small boys are no longer sent up chimneys and there are laws about chemical pollutants we assume that industrial circumstances have been universally transformed for the better. But this is a global world where rickety factories out east house underpaid and underfed armies of workers tied by debt to their employers. We also rejoice in the strong place women now hold in Western society, yet are living with massive people-trafficking and the proliferation of violent pornography. How are we to measure progress in such situations?

The fact is, some things get better and some get worse; the current state of affairs in Syria can scarcely be called an improvement on anything; the gross abuse of women by certain religions awaits the arrival of progress at any level. On the other hand, medical research continues improving to an almost miraculous degree; neuroscience is exploring the nature of our consciousness; astronomy is leaping ahead with discoveries about universes that can only be greeted as astounding; and our concern for the planet and the future of flora and fauna has a strong foothold in the minds of many.

There is one small area of human activity that concerns me. It is of apparently trivial import, but the bedrock of commercial wealth on a global scale. It touches each of us in our daily lives: indeed we could hardly dress, eat, furnish our homes, bring up our families, take holidays or enjoy leisure without a sense of its deadly grip. It is the emergence of brands, the identifying mark that has overtaken the old-fashioned nature of goods.

Brands have now become the identifying attribute of each and every thing. And not just things. I was told by someone in the BBC that at their annual interview where future prospects are discussed they were seriously advised to 'improve your brand image'. Branding is what makes for commercial success – in objects, companies, individuals, political parties, charities and presumably countries. Brands are a smart way of offering a doctored truth to the world; to what extent it reflects reality you will only know when you've bought in to the offer.

Brands, as the powerful marketing device they are today, have emerged within my lifetime. It wasn't always like this. Certainly I can scour my cupboards now and come up with labels that tell me: Twinings – since 1706. Hoover, invented in 1908 in Ohio, became so famous with its 1919 slogan 'It beats ... as it sweeps ... as it cleans' that before long the word 'hoover' became the colloquial way to refer to vacuum cleaners. 'Guinness is good for you' looked down from the hoardings on my way to school. At that time, Guinness was the seventh-largest company in the world; it still leads the world market for stout, though its advertising promising health benefits is now illegal.

There were relatively few brands with such global status until the mid-twentieth century. It was then advertising caught up with manufacturing as a major industry. The growth of branding was on its way. I worked as a copywriter in the global advertising agency McCann Erickson at the height of its *Mad Men* fame. And I saw at first hand how branding worked. I was one of the team working on the Esso petrol account and the word came from its American powerhouse headquarters that we were to test-market a new slogan. Long research documents explaining the psychology of car owning, of speed and of motoring style were produced. It all seemed pretty obvious stuff to me, but long and thoughtful meetings were held to consider the direction the advertising should take. The eventual headline – Put a Tiger in Your Tank – was clearly meant to appeal to aggressive male drivers and was played out in a variety of jokey, cartoonish advertisements. Perhaps the young Jeremy Clarkson glimpsed it from his cradle.

On the domestic front things were slower to get going. I had grown up in a world where you went to the grocer's and asked for a pound of butter (or, more likely, a half-pound in view of rationing). The grocer would then cut a chunk from a huge mound of butter on a marble slab, judging its weight by eye, place it upon a sheet of greaseproof paper then on another sheet of blue absorbent paper and pat it into shape with two wooden paddles with ridged surfaces. Only when it looked like all the other helpings he made was he satisfied and the whole thing packaged up and put on the scales. Bacon was likewise sold from the piece: a range of sides waiting for us to choose the cut, and then have it cut at the required thickness slice by painstaking slice. The same procedure followed at the butcher's: the customer would be offered a choice of cuts taken from huge carcasses hanging in the cold room and cut exactly to individual requirements. Each piece was tailor-made for each particular family, plus a selection of black pudding, chitterlings, hearts, liver, tripe and kidneys. This was all hugely time-consuming and especially problematic as at each shop there would be a queue of housewives waiting their turn to be served. There was no mass packaging and shopping was a slow, almost leisurely business. Often it would take my mother all morning, and she would be shopping again the next day. Being a housewife was a full-time occupation with none of the short cuts that now make it possible for women to have a paid job as well.

Then came packaging and supermarkets. It's hard to imagine now how many complaints there were among my mother's generation that they wouldn't enjoy personal service any longer and what a burden it put on the shopper to collect their own goods when really the effort belonged to the grocer – or greengrocer, or butcher. Besides, how were they to differentiate between the increasing torrent of packaged goods? Once there was just milk and butter and cheese and tins of beans – always Heinz. Suddenly customers used to being waited on were required to do their own fetching and carrying. How were they ever to make head or tail of what they wanted? How were they to know what they wanted? That, of course, is where advertising came in. Advertising would tell them. Advertising would de-skill them of their judgement.

And so the goods poured into the shops and the advertisements poured into the papers and magazines and onto television. Commercials became the new arena for lively creative people to work in: David Puttnam, Alan Parker, Fay Weldon, even Salman Rushdie all polished their verbal and visual skills in the service of Mammon. I used to love the Monday-morning sessions in the agency's viewing room when all the week's newest commercials were transmitted to subscribing advertising agencies. It was all quite larky and fun, with a good deal of *Mad Men* posturing going on.

But branding has got out of hand. If it was ever seen as serving the interests of the consumer that time has now gone. Chain stores and supermarkets are branded, garages, individual shops, even banks have logos and slogans that bear little relation to the way they are run or the goods they sell. Of all the domestic services we use perhaps only hairdressing – despite the Vidal Sassoon salon revolution of the 1960s – remains a matter for small businesses dependent on a local clientele and surviving on their reputation rather than heavy branding and slogans . . . a perfect arena for independent young women to set up their own businesses.

It would be good if the same applied to clothes. I would love to find a shop called The Coat Shop, which sold nothing but coats, racks of coats, all styles, all sizes, all colours. How helpful that would be when what you want is nothing more nor less than a coat. Instead, wanting a coat and being able to choose from a substantial selection means trawling through different concessions and franchises in each of the department stores or moving along the high street seeing a coat or two in each of the many fashion shops, each with their own brand and logo. Or you can do the same online, but you still have to access a whole host of websites, printing out or holding in your memory the style of each of the ones you fancy. This system was not conceived in the interest of the consumer: it has evolved from the emerging power of the brands, much happier to herd us into shops where every item carries their own label. Shopping power lies in the shops rather than those of us who know what we want and just need to know where to find it.

Eiderdown into duvet

Once there was a skill to making a bed. It was exact but time-consuming. Mothers taught daughters; male members of the family had it done for them. It was always cited as the hospital bed method: sheets top and bottom, tightly tucked in, the top sheet folded at the bottom of the bed with geometric precision into a triangle that was then tucked below the mattress at end and sides with suffocating rigour. This sheet would stay in place until the time came for the whole bed to be changed: it gave little space for movement. It wasn't meant to: it resembled those swaddling clothes that pinion the arms of small babies to their sides in medieval paintings. Above the sheets were two blankets, sometimes satin-edged, sometimes finished with the appropriately named blanket stitch. They too were tucked in firmly and unyieldingly, fixing the baby, the child, in place. Above them rested the soft and yielding texture of the eiderdown, the crowning glory of the bed, which in a time when there was no central heating sealed the warmth within. In honour of its looser feel and often pretty colours it was not tucked in, not tucked in at all. I thought, as a child, that this was the universal and only correct way to make a bed. Children make such assumptions.

And then I went to Austria. At first, on going to my room, I thought there had been a mistake and my bed was unmade. There seemed to be a heap like a giant meringue lying in the middle of the mattress. No one had done any tucking in. Something was wrong.

In her lovely book *The Making of Home*, Judith Flanders traces the history of houses and rooms, and also soft furnishings, through the centuries and explains how we come to have the homes we have today. Bedrooms, she writes, were once as much public rooms as the rest of the house, where the rich displayed their wealth in expensive four-poster beds hung with heavy tapestries on display for all to admire. Much, I imagine, as tourists gape in disbelief at the lavish bedrooms on guided tours through stately homes. Jan van Eyck's Arnolfini Portrait of 1434 includes an imposing four-poster draped with red curtains, a demonstration of the family wealth. Madame de Maintenon, the second wife of Louis XIV, undressed and slept in the room where the king and his ministers were meeting. No wonder they had heavy curtains.

It was in the eighteenth century that things began to change, with greater privacy and less flamboyance. Of course the ordinary people had never enjoyed such luxury, being content, in earlier centuries, to hunker down on a sack filled with straw in any place they could find. But as society got wealthy, families – even modest families – began to spend more than half their wealth on beds, bedding and clothing. Bedding was one of the earliest consumer goods: in the seventeenth century up to a third of a Dutch household's worth might be invested in bedding; by the eighteenth century, up to 40 per cent of a working family's wealth.

More generally, up to a quarter of all expenditure on

household goods would be laid out on bedding. Those stuffed sacks were piled high, one on top of another, as the concept of comfort took hold. Ms Flanders then goes on to give a lyrical account of how things got better:

> with different types of bedding becoming available – bolsters, pillows, sheets, blankets, various types of covers, spreads and quilts. And then came improvement in quality: straw was replaced by hemp or flock stuffing, and then by wool; feathers ranged from down, to goosedown, to eider, while from the eighteenth century, factory-manufactured cotton waste was also available; finer wool blankets replaced felted ones; and flax and linen replaced coarse canvas.

No one mentions duvets.

But that's not quite so: in the mid-eighteenth century Thomas Nugent, an Englishman on a grand tour, passed through Westphalia and noted:

> There is one thing very particular to them, that they do not cover themselves with bed-clothes, but lay one feather-bed over, and another under. This is comfortable enough in winter, but how they can bear their feather-beds over them in summer, as is generally practised, I cannot conceive.

Clearly no one had yet thought of togs.

Thomas Nugent went on to relate this anecdote:

> When the French Protestants were obliged, in the last century, to quit their country, the Swiss, in particular, received

those who took shelter among them with the greatest hospitality. Some poor Frenchmen being conducted to their bedchamber, one of them espying a feather-bed over, and another under, imagined that there was a design to make them lie one upon another for want of room. Upon which he addressed himself to the servant, and desired him to choose one of his lightest companions to put over him, alleging that he was not accustomed to lie in this manner.

Even startled as I was by my Austrian meringue, I never thought that such an arrangement was intended for me.

In setting out the timeline of household change Judith Flanders makes clear that my own place is just behind the present day. My comfort zone, where I first learned about the world, its habits and its values, lurks at ease in the second half of the twentieth century. That is the age that bore me and nurtured me, that formed the trajectory of my life and times. And though of course I live in the present and I enjoy many of its benefits – medical improvements, personal informality, mutual tolerance between generations, the abundance of goods that make life easy and pleasant – I am not quite as deeply at home here as I felt myself to be at an earlier age. Though my bed enjoys the latest comfort and making it calls for nothing more than a shrug and a throw, I am clearly a pre-duvet person.

Sherry into lager

If I didn't have the evidence I would find it hard to believe it was true. But I have the proof in black and white: my generation of Cambridge students drank sherry. Sherry! Oh, we drank beer and wine and martini and brandy and gin and all those other things too, of course. But the social drink of choice was sherry.

Because I am such a hoarder I don't have to depend on memory, which so often plays us false, especially about those golden days of youth. I stashed away long ago and have scarcely re-examined since much of the detritus of student life: the annual university handbook, membership of clubs. There are letters from parents asking why I haven't written more often, programmes for theatre productions, exam papers in both the economics and the history tripos. And a small stack of party invitations. It is these that tell the story.

First they are all the same size, a modest three inches by four: neat, white, no variations, no inventive student creativity. Second, many of them are printed, some in the traditional 'At Home' variety. Others decorously 'Request the Pleasure'. A number – the posher sort – have the name of the host or hosts individually printed too. There is one, just one, that holds a glimpse of student wit and non-conformity. T. S. Eliot was all the rage and a spirited wedding invitation came in the form of a pastiche: '. . . As they change their station / They pass the stages of their age and youth / Entering the whirl-pool.' Otherwise they were dull and quite content to mirror the world of adults whose style and values dominated the taste and look of the world we lived in. Students as a genre hadn't yet come into being. Teenagers were still in the future. I caught a glimpse of what was on its way when I was excit-edly invited to a party to hear a recording of some new kind of music. It was Bill Haley's 'Rock Around the Clock'. But I couldn't imagine what the future might be like and would probably have been alarmed if I had. Rock, together with drugs, was to arrive in the decade that followed.

Our choice of sherry may well have been copied from the adult world familiar to many of my fellow students. They often came from genteel homes where I can imagine a glass of sherry being proffered before Sunday lunch. In my own home we had a single bottle of sweet sherry tucked away in a cupboard and only brought out at Christmas. It lasted us several years. I had my first taste of drink when I was taken out by schoolboys who would buy me a gin and orange or gin and It (Italian vermouth). At Cambridge one knew to beware on nights of rugby club revelry when, on one occasion, I remember all the street lamps being decked with hanging bicycles taken from the unlocked stacks left outside colleges. And I was truly shocked when, partying on a boat on the Cam, someone took a wind-up gramophone and flamboyantly tossed it into the river. Post-war austerity made such abandon reckless indeed. In the 1950s ours was not a hard-drinking culture and it came as a shock in my first year at Cambridge to go to parties, the entire purpose of which was to drink and talk. To drink sherry. And, of course, smoke. I had some rough experiences in those first weeks but never got the hang of how drinking to excess was meant to be a pleasure. I also became a smoker.

Drinking to excess has long since become the prevailing nature of student life; students drink to excess and enjoy it. Binge drinking is their idea of fun, at least for many. Initiation ceremonies of gruelling levels of intoxication characterise freshers' weeks. There are challenges of ever more extreme bouts and the routine of hangovers has to be taken into consideration by lecturers working the early morning shift. In university cities, residents have come to expect that on Friday and Saturday nights certain areas are well avoided. And the police are regularly under pressure to deal with violence or simply cart away bodies lying in the gutter.

We live in times when people measure and judge others' behaviour. Surveys and focus groups attempt to offer numbers where once there was only speculation. Drink is now a matter of units. Today we know what Cambridge students actually drink from an item in their newspaper, *Varsity*, of January 2015. It revealed that the average student regularly exceeds recommended limits and that over half have missed academic commitments as a consequence. Nobody bothered recommending limits in my day, so it would be harsh to assume that the situation has worsened, though there is plenty of anecdotal evidence that it has. The abundance of drinking societies sets the tone: think of the Bullingdon at Oxford as a classic bad example. Nowadays almost half of all Cambridge students claim to have been a member of a drinking society at some time during their time at university. Is there an explanation for this level of drinking other than a hefty thirst? Do these societies bulk-buy liquor at bargain rates? Or is the pressure of university so great they need to seek oblivion?

I see that I am trying to find excuses for student behaviour rather than condemning it. That's because it's so easy and regular a response of the older generation to deplore what the young get up to, and an it-wasn't-like-that-in-my-day attitude is both too facile and far from intelligent. As I'm busy demonstrating, virtually nothing was the same in my day: the nature of change means we oldies simply can't know what it is to be young in today's world. And it's not our fault.

And yet I have to regret it. When I look to the world that the young will inherit, I don't want it to be a place where binge drinking is the norm; where alcohol-related illnesses bulk large. I notice that in other cultures alcohol is either forbidden or sparingly used. I would like some of their abstemiousness to spread. It may be that a culture shift is needed in the West and will have, at the start, to be government-directed, with for example higher taxes on drink and a minimum pricing policy. If we have managed to make cigarette smoking unacceptable, we can surely change the way we view alcohol. But in the end such a shift will have to be willingly embraced. To forbid it is to glamorise; to criminalise is to create criminals. Prohibition brought the era of the bootleggers and Al Capone.

And there is much of benefit from drinking. I know personally that alcohol is a pleasure; that the variety of its forms and tastes brings delight and satisfaction. Being alive is to respond to the fruits of the earth in all their numerous manifestations. It would be negative and dictatorial to drive out one of its conspicuous and subtle rewards. So may the vines flourish, the hops grow strong and the people rejoice . . . in moderation.

Handwriting – keyboards

I have two letters from 1959 written by my grandfather, then eighty-three years old. He was writing to congratulate me on the birth of my daughter – 'it is a wonderful achievement to reach motherhood'. He must have learned to read and write in the 1880s, at a local school where he grew up in Burton upon Trent. He was a big, rough man with the horny hands of toil supposedly so characteristic of the working class. They were big gnarled hands, that grabbed me and sat me on his knee, so he could brush his whiskery chin across my pale cheek . . . and laugh. Not a sophisticated man.

But his handwriting was immaculate Victorian copperplate. Each word is exactly formed, the lines straight on unlined paper, the loops of ys and gs, of hs and bs all regularly and evenly shaped. The capital letters are allowed a special flourish, a curly sweep to the D and a pleasing swirl on the A . This is writing with care: an old man taking time to fill the page and then sign off, 'is the sincere wish of your loving Grandad'.

I have boxes and boxes of letters, all written by hand. I can tell whom they are from by the handwriting: my mother's long and sloping heavily forward, my father's trim and exact. My Cambridge friends dropping notes about this and that – there were no phones we could easily use – were hugely characteristic: Karl Miller's bold explosive letters, Peter Hall's neat and rounded, Michael Bakewell's tight and intense, Harry Guest's close and ornate. Even today I can identify the writer.

I recently passed on to my son my hoard of the memorabilia of his life. I had kept all his reports from the 1960s, notebooks, early drawings (mothers do that sort of thing). The exercise books showed him practising his letters: neat rows of As then neat rows of Bs . . . all the way through the alphabet, then the joining up of one letter to another. I recall myself the excitement, back in my own childhood, when the teacher said 'and today we're going to start on "joined-up"'. How thrilling could life be as a learning child.

Today there is every reason to suppose it is more exciting than ever: early on the winking lights and coloured buttons of electronic toys, at school the transition to computers, laptops and all the variety of electronic communications. Finally the emerging student, in touch with the world at the flick of a finger, emailing, texting, attaching, exchanging selfies, up-to-the-minute with Facebook and Twitter, electronic games being played across continents. No wonder handwriting is neglected and letter-writing a lost art.

Does it matter? Not a lot. It is merely one of the old crafts falling into disuse because the need is no long there. I regret it – as I regret the loss of hand-loom weaving, and jam-making. Not much. Then I wonder, would Virginia Woolf have sent emails? and more importantly would Strachey and Keynes et al. have saved them? The world could have been a poorer place.

Hats into hoodies

We courted detention after school hours if we were seen in school uniform but without our hats. I had the choice between a brimmed navy felt hat with the school colours – navy and gold – on the ribbon and an elastic band under your chin, or a small woollen cap rather like a beanie with a metal school badge pinned at the front. From the age of fifteen we were in rebellion against all uniform, but our protests were puny. We seized the chance to invent our own style, making modest protest against the conformity being imposed on us. We did this by folding pleats so deep in the felt of our hats that they needed two hat pins to hold them on the back of our heads. The trendiest girls had the most precarious hats. We had plenty of hat pins, of course. Our mothers needed them: they always wore hats. Even for shopping. You weren't considered dressed without one.

Covering the head has been a usual part of dress for centuries. Why wouldn't it be, with the outdoor life more commonly exposed to rain and sun than today? As a child I wore hats that matched my little-girl coats, confections of velvet and worsted, and pixy hoods knitted by generous aunts and grannies. My mother wore felt or straw hats according to season. They were plain and substantial rather than frilled and flowered, covering against the weather,

The Whit Walk. I am second from left: new hat, new gloves, new shoes and socks

practical and unstylish. Women were expected to wear hats at church, hats that for special occasions might be decked with flowers and veiling. I always loved veiling: it had glamour and mystery. I'm surprised it hasn't returned in the way of fashion revivals.

Going without a hat therefore became a gesture of rebellion, a way of defying convention. Hairdressers loved it because it gave scope to a new art, that of styling. I gave up my plaits for soft waves, fixed into place by permanent-wave chemicals and metal curlers. But my hair fell into limp strands in the Stockport drizzle. Hats clearly had their uses.

By the 1960s no one – apart from royals and dignitaries and women at race meetings – wore serious hats. There was a sudden vogue for large floppy hats but it was too impractical to last. Besides, hair had come into its own. Hairdressing emerged as a serious profession. Peroxide gave way to softer chemical hair dyes and pop stars – not all of them female – led the way with startling colours and lengths. I shared the infectious fun that went along with it.

But the weather was still cold and wet. Social norms softened and so did the fabrics. New garments were invented: the windcheater evolved into the hoodie; various plastics morphed into showerproofs; people were so quickly in and out of cars and buildings that no one used gloves any more, except in the coldest weather. Fashion keen to promote its growing market invented trendiness and extremes; high prices became the arbiter of good taste, yet people with little money could look good on very little. Young people desperate for individuality ended up looking much like one another. But freedom was all. The days of conformity and convention are well rid of.

Ravel to reggae

For me it began with shellac recordings played on wind-up gramophones. Since then, the revolution. I have seen music transformed. Now it's everywhere, of every style and perpetually available. It's hard to persuade younger people it wasn't always like this. But look back in time and Beethoven never heard performances of his works. I don't refer to his deafness, but to the fact they weren't performed. Berlioz never heard his great opera *The Trojans*, Bruckner never heard his Symphony No. 5. Music simply was not as available as it is now: each composer, each piece needed a promoter, an orchestra, a concert hall and a public. Times and technology have changed all that. Music is more widely enjoyed, explored and distributed than ever before.

My parents had a wind-up gramophone, purchased on their trip to Argentina in 1938; I have it still. It has a velvet-surfaced turntable, an articulated arm with a stylus that holds gramophone needles. A little dish beside the turntable is for replacements and discards.

The few records they collected were of 1930s dance music, with the occasional crooner barely audible through the scratchy sounds of the record.

In the 1950s we graduated to a radiogram, a bulky piece of furniture walnut-faced and taking up the entire bay window. We had a collection of classical music on 78 records; the first I actually purchased with my own pocket money was Tchaikovsky's Piano Concerto No. 1 in B flat minor: I inclined to gushing romantic sounds with strong rhythm and lots of noise. (Ennio Morricone grew up in the decades I did and our lives would converge in the 1980s when I reported on the making of the film *The Mission*.) I still like romantic sounds with strong rhythm and lots of crescendos. Buying a recording was a major event in our household. It didn't happen often and records were regarded as special treats, as though exposure to too many of them too often would coarsen our taste.

Rosemary and Betty Clooney sing 'Sisters': a gift from Susan to me

Instead we had the radio: *Housewives' Choice* and *Forces Favourites*. Roy Plomley's *Desert Island Discs* came along in January 1942, feeding the new concept of single individuals with a range of personal tastes we might share. And then in 1946 came the Third Programme, dedicated in rather high-minded tones to classical music. Too high-minded for my parents, so we didn't often listen. The range and capacity of listening even in homes that professed to like classical music was strictly limited. Our household, like most others, would own just one radiogram, combining radio and record player, so parental tastes prevailed, and the listening was confined to one room, the living room, which was in those days the only room to have any heating, and that from a coal fire in the grate.

Change in taste went hand in hand with technology. With my teenage years came the free-standing record player, and I began to collect records of my own and play them in my own room, defiantly putting up with the cold to assert my independence. Again soupy tastes prevailed: the *Warsaw Concerto* and music from *The Glass Mountain*. From films I also picked up a taste for American songs – *Meet Me in St Louis* and *Easter Parade*. Home-grown taste ran to Johnnie Ray and Adam Faith. And a meagre selection of classical music: I have some of those 78s today and the sound quality is so poor it's not hard to see why I failed to understand the subtleties of classical composition. For that I had to trek to Manchester to hear the legendary Hallé orchestra, in those days conducted by Sir John Barbirolli and playing at the now-demolished Free Trade Hall. The point is music was hard to find; listening to records had its family and social inconveniences, and live music needed real effort.

Music and its enjoyment is one of the great creative movements of our time. The tide of musical enthusiasm and creative passion that swept into the 1960s began the shift. But even then it depended on what was available. In Liverpool youngsters begged records off the crews – many of them friends and relations – serving on the ocean liners going to and from New York. Merchant seamen came and went, bringing prized copies of jazz and blues, Chuck Berry and Bill Haley. Young people got together in homes where they could play; they began to buy guitars of their own. And that did it! What had been Liverpool jazz venues began to welcome rock and roll. The Beatles colonised the Cavern. The city was seized by a passion of creativity: at one time there were four hundred groups playing there.

Then, famously, at Dartford railway station on 17 October 1961 Mick Jagger, carrying his blues records, bumped into Keith Richards carrying his guitar and got talking about music. From the meeting came the Rolling Stones, still, more than fifty years later, playing and touring with the music that changed the musical landscape.

My life was going through its own awakening. By the mid-1960s I was working on *Late Night Line-Up*, BBC Television's late-night discussion programme: seven days a week on BBC 2, right round the year; the only holiday was Christmas Day. Such a schedule needed a lot of filling – only the daily news exceeds it in regular commitment. We seized the chance to broadcast as widely and as eclectically as we could. Music was a natural favourite, and because with only three channels the opportunities to broadcast were limited, musicians, groups and soloists were eager for the air time we could give them. And we didn't stint. Along came the Kinks, the Bee Gees, Lionel Richie, Joni Mitchell, Elton John. But also, and usually given to me as their interviewer, came classical music's avant-garde: Luciano Berio, Karlheinz Stockhausen, Pierre Boulez, John Cage.

They too were interested in pushing the bounds of technology, and none more so than John Cage, who virtually pushed them over a cliff. His 4'33" is an orchestral piece in three movements which has no actual music at all. Both orchestra and audience sit in total silence, each listening to the ambient noise and hearing silence in his or her own way. John Cage was delighted to be invited on the programme but, as is appropriate to his unique approach to performance, didn't want to talk about music at all. 'Let's talk about cooking,' he suggested. *Line-Up* and I were quite happy to go along with the idea and I remember him describing to me an Armenian recipe in which an entire chicken was enfolded in salt before being baked. There was much laughter and exchanging of culinary gossip.

At the time there was little control exercised by a BBC hierarchy to challenge what we were doing, and only any official post mortem when we had gone too far. Those days – in terms of music, creativity and technology – were freer from the constraints of officialdom, and were comfortable with playing with ideas. Today the world of creative energy struggles against forces of money, bureaucracy and ratings to enjoy its freedom.

Soon the technology would outflank me. LPs gave way to CDs gave way to iPods and earbuds. At this point I halted and let the horses race on without me. My ears have never taken to earbuds. I can handle headphones, but that is not the point. I like to hear music in the natural acoustic of where I am listening. I know perfectly well that a CD of an orchestra recorded in a concert hall is not the acoustic of my living room. But the ambient sound of where I am matters as part of my musical experience. John Cage would agree.

So I leave behind me a spare selection of favourite vinyl; a couple of shelves of CDs and the Beatles' original recording of *Sgt. Pepper* – the one everyone has. It won't be how people listen to music in future, so they're probably for the tip.

Come to think of it, perhaps I'll have *Sgt. Pepper* in the coffin with me. To those who come after I bequeath increasing conflicts over internet copyright, charges of plagiarism and the growing power of showbiz moguls to manipulate talented hopefuls taking their chance on television shows. But somehow the music will transcend it all.

Bisto to quinoa

Food in my time has developed in a multitude of different directions: GM crops, the organic movement, microwaves, high-street takeaways, restaurant porn, cookery books, diet crazes and illnesses such as diabetes and obesity. Much of our media focuses on cooking and eating and its wider ramifications: the catering industry, medical fall-out, global crop scarcities and gluts. As with the stuff itself, we just can't get enough of it.

Once it was considered shameful to eat food in the street, so it rarely happened. If I bought fish and chips on the way home from Brownies I kept quiet about it, and washed the greasy smell from my hands as soon as I got home. The secrecy made the transgression all the more fun, and I still recall the particular tang of chips and vinegar eaten under the bright wintery moon. Pleasure in food was rare and snatched on the quiet. Rationing stayed in force even into the 1950s.

The purpose of food was simply different in those days. It was primarily regarded as nutrition served up at three specific times a day to fuel the human body and keep it running. In the north of England, the evening meal served at around six o'clock was called tea: 'Have you had your tea?' would be the first question when a friend called round or rang to share some gossip. Elsewhere in the country it was, depending on your class, supper or dinner. But schoolchildren all signed up to school dinners at midday, cooked in the school's own kitchens by professional dinnerladies in white overalls. Packed lunches came later, when children got fads and parents indulged them.

Meals were routine, the same every Monday and so on through the week, both at home and at school. They were solid and satisfying: we were not allowed to leave anything on our plates. There were hungry children, we were told, who would be glad of what we were refusing. There were many stand-offs with refusenik children kept back, sitting chewing for hours after the table had been cleared. If some foods were tasty that was simply a bonus: Granny's fruit cake was delicious, the skin on rice pudding was repellent. I swallowed both. Meals were eaten at home with the observation of certain rituals. We had serviettes changed weekly and kept in silver rings with names engraved on them. I still have the one given to me as a christening present. We each sat in our own place round the table, and when we had finished we were expected to ask 'Please may I leave the table?' The answer could be 'No', unless there was homework to be done.

This rather dour regime was repetitive and unvaried. Monday would be shepherd's or cottage pie using minced leftovers from Sunday's joint of meat; Tuesday sausages and grilled tomatoes; Wednesday macaroni cheese; Thursday potato pie (stewed meat folded into mashed potatoes under a pastry lid with lashings of gravy); Friday, fried fish and chips; Saturday sliced ham and salad with Heinz salad cream. A plate of bread and butter was served with every meal and a cake stand with home-made scones and cakes stood at the corner of the table for when – and only if – we had cleared our plates. There was to be no waste. Nor were there concessions to taste: everyone was served the same plate of food; to be a vegetarian was simply eccentric and not indulged. No one was allowed to voice preferences, likes and dislikes. So it never occurred to us. That wasn't the point of food. We grew up knowing it was simply a part of the household's daily routine and how things were.

The world of food and of eating has since been convulsed with change, all of it in the direction of ever-extending variety and more and more pleasure. It has been such an extraordinary journey for me. I have at every stage fallen hook, line and sinker for the latest trends. In the post-war years came the shock of foreign food. During the war fruit had meant apples and pears and sometimes home-grown raspberries and redcurrants. And yes, I believe I remember the first bananas arriving from the West Indies. At least I think I remember, though the tale has been told so often and by so many different people that I could have adopted the account into my own recollections. Memories are like that: they need backing with fact. I go exploring my youthful diaries – yes, it's there. January 29th 1946: 'I had my first banana for six years.'

I was a young wife and mother in the 1960s, completely in love with all the new foods – aubergine, endive, avocado – and with Elizabeth David's books that told of the warm south as much as the way to cook. For the first time in my life food became a display activity and we gave dinner parties with fancy dishes, candlelight, after-dinner mints and good wine. I found the whole thing exhausting of body and spirit, and was glad when restaurant eating became the fashion.

Then in the 1980s food became political. Band Aid was pop music's response to the crisis in Ethiopia: a single individual, Bob Geldof, was so moved by the plight of starving children he rallied his pop music contacts to produce a charity record. In 1984 'Do They Know It's Christmas?' went straight to the top of the UK charts, selling a million copies in the first week alone. It went on, in different incarnations, to raise money and awareness of starvation worldwide. Feed the World became its tagline, prompting other celebrity fundraisers, the start of Live Aid and continuing into Band Aid 30 re-recording the song with different pop stars and offering aid to the victims of the 2014 Ebola outbreak in West Africa.

Thus were global needs – first for food, and then medical supplies – met with the passionate response of musicians who used their celebrity to make something happen.

Today we have ludicrous extremes: fancy food of great extravagance served in dinky portions for huge sums; food banks in our cities for families going short; famine across tracts of the world beset by wars; magazines and books promoting ever more extravagant and unlikely ingredients; and crops grown in Israel and Kenya flown across the planet to serve the tables of the UK. How simple it all was before diversity arrived. We never went hungry, plenty did. But we knew it was wrong and hoped it would change.

Now the tables of the rich stagger under the weight of new concoctions, the latest silly menus; the poor battle at the tailgates of lorries for a cup of emergency rice. Something isn't right. Progress has a funny way of panning out.

Discipline to indulgence

It was usual in my childhood for parents to smack their children; it was common, unremarked, accepted. But my mother was quick to do so. Whatever was to hand – slipper, hairbrush, belt – I would be taken to my bedroom and given it. It simply made me more subversive and stubborn than ever. And I resolved when I became a parent to be different. Come the 1960s, when my children were born, the chance was waiting for me.

Dr Benjamin Spock published his book *Baby and Child Care* in 1946 and for the next fifty-two years it was the world's second-best seller after the Bible. In the 1960s I myself wore out two copies. Dr Spock was a game changer. First of all he was American, from the golden land of informality and laughter. We saw as much in the movies. No wonder we fell for Spock. Suddenly children of 1960s parents flourished in new ways – relaxed and easy-going, comfortable with grown-ups and the world around them. I like to believe mine were among them. I was happy to set aside the inhibitions and repressions of my parents. Feminism was dawning. My generation of mothers was starting to combine jobs and maternity, and also seeking to shape the future of our sons so they would emerge as adults more in sympathy with the aspirations of women. Early feminists like Erin Pizzey declared that for women to have an equal life we must break with the traditional way of bringing up our sons. I remember buying my son a doll, one that had genitals; it was all part of helping to shape the new way men would behave. And indeed it proved so: in the eras since, dads have become more closely involved in caring, often attendant at the birth and able and willing to push buggies and change nappies. It has been a major social shift of my lifetime and one that rejoices my heart. It's a joy to see young fathers taking such tender care of their children, holding, touching, caressing them . . . expressing the love that helps them flourish.

But the prevailing outlook of the times left space for error. Tolerance could drift for some towards indifference, 'relaxed' could degenerate into 'uninvolved'. Sometimes, without intent, family life descended into chaos, parents unable to cope with the assertive demands and needs of their children. Unhappily, many women were confused, and sometimes I was one of them. Yes, I wanted my children to have all the freedom of action and expression that the liberal teaching extolled. But in practice I still wanted my children to learn to behave in ways that made family life civilised. I was keen on mealtimes and table manners, listening when others were talking and not crashing around hurting others and damaging things. I was in no-man's-land between the permissives and the controllers. But what I thought of as progress doesn't go on going forward: in the decades that followed there was a swing of the pendulum. Help arrived with the sort of child-rearing mantras that would redress the balance. Books by professional child nurses like Gina Ford and 'Supernanny' Jo Frost, and Amy Chua's *Battle Hymn of the Tiger Mother* promoted strictness and discipline of the old school. You made your choice.

Meanwhile another discipline – this time an academically based theory – was making its way into the hearts and minds of parents. As a young mother in the early 1960s I had been alarmed by the widely publicised findings of John Bowlby. I wasn't the only one. Bowlby was a heavyweight

British psychologist and psychiatrist who wrote a report on the mental health of homeless children in post-war Europe. The result – *Maternal Care and Mental Health* – was published in 1951, a mere handful of years before I was to embark on marriage and having children. Bowlby concluded that unless a child experienced 'a warm, intimate and continuous relationship with his mother' there could be significant and irreversible mental health consequences.

How bad could that be?

Then, decades later, the theory emerged again, as 'attachment parenting'. This time, the language was less one of negative and dire warnings but a positive and upbeat promotion of perpetual and undeviating care. Attachment parenting has become a strong and widely endorsed family practice, with even working parents taking care that any carers they appoint are as sensitive to their child's needs as they are. This is indeed a tall order. Young children – even when you adore them and want their lives to be perfect – are often taxing, irritating, awkward and contrary.

Parenting continues to be a bigger issue than ever. It now mirrors the highly competitive nature of today's society. It is in that vein that mothers and fathers want to succeed as parents and set the evidence before the world. Too often offspring rank alongside a nice house, good car and successful career as a measure of how others judge you and how you judge yourself. Scruffy, delinquent children mark out your failure. Parenting has been commodified as a measure of individual success.

The competition starts in pregnancy: how good are you at being pregnant? In my day it wasn't something you considered.

You got pregnant, told the local GP, gave notice you would be leaving your job (no such thing as maternity leave or maternity pay) and coped on your own with morning sickness. Now the pregnancy police are out to get you: soft cheeses, pâtés are forbidden, drinking and smoking completely outlawed. The whole childbearing enterprise is elevated into an achievers' nightmare with rules of behaviour and diet set to terrorise the most eager. Then, at the end of the course, a minimising of risks and the delivery of a healthy baby.

I smoked and drank through two pregnancies – the doctor even suggested that as I went into labour I celebrate with a glass of champagne. I had two healthy babies, one a breech birth (i.e. bottom end first) with little fuss made about what seemed a minor complication. Indeed I was volunteered during my labour to be an exam question for a group of students doing their midwifery practical. They were sent in one by one to examine and ask me about my condition. I whispered the answer to each of them in turn. Pregnancy hadn't become professionalised.

Now so-called helicopter parents hover relentlessly over their children's lives. They spur on their sporting efforts from the sidelines, they complain to teachers who don't give them high enough marks, put their children under pressure for things that should be a pleasure, demanding they pass exams for playing musical instruments, win badges for proficiency. Its consequences – disappointment, anxiety, unhappiness – are the dark side of what began as loving devotion.

At the same time, in this highly judgemental society bad parenting is often blamed for low self-esteem, drug addiction, road rage (temper tantrums writ large), unhappy marriage, bad manners, lack of empathy, criminal tendencies, cheating when you don't expect to be found out. People – politicians mostly, goaded by members of the press – insist something must be done. They mean it at the time, but it turns out people are too busy.

So what do we pass on? What changes will endure? What swing of the pendulum comes next? Some things are certain. People in Britain will no longer smack their children: if they do with any force, they will end up before the magistrate. Women's working lives will mean that they will recruit others to help in bringing up their children. Such carers will struggle to have a higher status in the hierarchy of jobs. Parents will continue to be engulfed by experts and research offering them contradictory advice. There will be increasing loads of data and opinions derived from it. It will all be well meant.

But I see this over-emphasis on the child-centred family as offering a risky future. The way things are going, children's lives are increasingly micromanaged. The primary-school curriculum involves testing at earlier and earlier ages. Tests for numeracy and literacy are seen as drivers for a future workforce that supplies the labour for a growing economy. There doesn't seem much choice involved.

There isn't outside school either. Children are constrained, not allowed to wander off alone, to roam freely in open spaces where they can climb trees, collect frogspawn in local ponds, pick wild flowers, go blackberrying. The places where you can do such things are being fenced off. Private property and development are cutting young people off from their natural surroundings.

At the same time as the school curriculum gets more pre-scriptive it is also reducing opportunities for creativity and physicality. The learning that passes exams is not enough. Without free-ranging creativity – the chance to be wild and daring, to try new ways of being yourself – the human spirit is cramped. Having the choice to play music, sing in choirs, act in school plays, visit theatres and museums is an option increasingly under pressure from emphasis on the sterner stuff: science, technology, engineering and maths . . . the STEM subjects. School playgrounds are being sold off, children often have to travel further to play games, use cycle tracks, learn to swim. Those playgrounds won't easily be retrieved: they have been absorbed into the property develop-ers' world where any locations of civic worth – social housing, public spaces – have to be fought for against complicit planning authorities and the power of money.

I was lucky. Of course I was. After the war there were bombed-out buildings and no one bothered when gangs of kids went climbing and exploring. We came in from the great outdoors with red cheeks and torn clothes to settle to our homework. Mothers were fully occupied with washing, drying and ironing clothes, daily shopping, queuing and cooking. They left us to ourselves, and if strange men did odd things we were to run away and tell someone. Somehow it was no big deal.

Now everything is a big deal. If you don't pass exams your future is doomed; if you don't get to the right school, your first-choice university, you're already a failure in the world's eyes and, more damagingly, in your own. If a stranger puts his hand on your shoulder you must tell a policeman and be given counselling. The pressure on young people is frantic: depression, self-harm, even suicide are on the increase. That's in the data too.

Now I'm old I'm exercising again the freedoms I knew as a child: the freedoms not to be tied to work and schedules. To be and do with your time whatever you like. That's why I'm at the cottage, sitting, thinking, being, reviewing my times and imagining what trace I'll leave behind.

On Work

D own by the river I crane my neck to see beyond the full
green foliage of the bordering trees. Along the bank
where others' gardens reach to the water small jetties and
adjacent landing stages are gradually coming to life; wooden
chairs and tables are brought from winter storage to greet the
summer. By the time the horse chestnuts are ablaze I shall be
back in town, to watch them shed their petals on Primrose
Hill. Country or city, the summer is transforming life and
lives. And moving mine on.

———

I have never had what people call a career. It surprises them
when I say as much. But I think of a career as an anticipated intention to do or become something . . . doctor,
teacher, actor . . . and to follow up on that intention with a
deliberate sequence of training episodes – apprenticeships,
degrees – that lead towards that goal. Once the goal is
within reach the intention expands: doctors become con-
sultants, teachers become heads, actors become film stars.
There is a logical and emotional progression that makes

sense either from the outset or looking back. I have never made such a progression.

Instead I have plotted my way through a working life via a steady sequence of jobs chosen simply because I enjoyed them. They often overlapped with each other, or made a serendipitous pairing. Journalism and broadcasting obviously go well together and mean that cycles of feast or famine more or less even each other out. I have had a working life that approximates to what is now becoming the norm among younger people. I have picked and mixed my choices, taken breaks for holidays – unpaid – as I wished, sometimes even dreamt up schemes of my own. Very much come and gone as I pleased. Today it is called having a portfolio career. I just alighted on this way of working long ago and found it suited my temperament. I am still doing it.

So where did it all go right? At my girls' grammar school paid work was what women did between leaving school and marriage. Spinsters were considered unlucky to have been left on the shelf. The prevailing vocabulary was brutal, and driven home. When my headmistress announced to the school that I was going on a scholarship to Cambridge she added a rider: 'Remember, girls, however pleased we are for Joan, the true calling of a woman's life is to be a wife and mother.' Careers and sustained work were not on the agenda, unless, like her and most of my other teachers, you were a spinster.

There were plenty of silent endorsements of this life-view. At school we were divided into competing houses. They were named for women of achievement: Brontë, Austen, Gaskell, Slessor, Nightingale and Beale. Only one of them – Mrs Gaskell – wrote while she was married. We became familiar

Stockport High School for Girls: closed by the comprehensive revolution

with the stories of these women's lives, of course. And for those of us with even vague ambitions the news wasn't promising. We knew the Brontë sisters had struggled to be recognised, adopting the ambiguously androgynous names of Currer, Acton and Ellis Bell, while their feckless brother Branwell blew the chances he was given for a serious career . . . as an artist, as a railway clerk. We knew Jane Austen led a modest life among a family of boisterous brothers, becoming a favoured aunt and writing when she could at the famous desk behind the creaking door. We knew Florence Nightingale had a tough time nursing soldiers in the Crimean War and a tougher time reforming the nursing profession when she came home. We knew that Mary Slessor, called to be a Christian missionary in Africa, suffered life-long from the malaria she contracted early on. We mocked

Dorothea Beale along with her educationalist colleague Frances
Mary Buss in the rhyme:

> Miss Buss and Miss Beale,
> Cupid's darts do not feel.
> How different from us,
> Miss Beale and Miss Buss.

Between them these worthy women just about nailed
what we could look forward to by way of a career. We were
expected to admire their struggle. It was part of what successful women would have to face. And then there was of
course Mrs Gaskell, who had satisfied all my headmistress's
standards: she was not only satisfactorily married to a distinguished Manchester Unitarian minister and the mother of five
children, but also the acclaimed author of six novels, shoals of
short stories and a renowned biography of her friend Charlotte
Brontë. So perhaps there was hope after all. At which point a
generation of young women embarked on a campaign to 'have
it all' . . . marriage, motherhood and career. A struggle that
in less strenuous ways persists to this day.

I had already, as a schoolgirl, learned what I did not want to
do. I had served cream teas each weekend to visitors to the
Deanwater Hotel. As the 'weekend relief' we were not a particularly fastidious group and there was no overseer. I recall
spilling a plate of cakes face down on the carpet and simply
picking them up, dusting them down and proceeding to the
customers in the lounge. The sense of service was missing;
what mattered was the tip. I was paid a pound a day. Later

I worked as a waitress in a café on Benllech Beach in North Wales. This was a bigger deal altogether: overnight accommodation and meals provided; boys in one dormitory, girls in another. I was reprimanded for being found in the boys' dormitory. It was daytime and an innocent call, but the owner saw himself as *in loco parentis* and was paternally angry.

What I learned was how rude and disobliging the public could be. I was a timid schoolgirl doing her best and any waitress knows she is at the mercy of the kitchen. If the kitchen delivers the food late it is the waiting staff who suffer. Again I lived for the tips . . . and found them unkindly withheld if the next table was served first – 'We were here before them!' I knew I didn't want to work on that front line.

Next to be eliminated: stolidly routine work. I worked one entire school holiday in an office of Manchester Education Department, tabulating by hand piles and piles of exam papers. Other friends were doing it too, so there was chat to relieve the monotony. But the repetitive work and its unrelenting pressure began to affect my brain. After only a few days I knew my capacity to think was slowing down. I responded sluggishly to any change in schedule. Ideas dried up. If this kind of tedium fell to those without any skills I knew I had better get on and pass some exams. It was a means of escape. I often wonder what the boredom of daily routine – in call centres, in offices, year in, year out – does to the minds of those who work there.

And here I am doing what is totally satisfying; the sort of job I always imagined. Sitting at the desk, writing away, allowing my mind to spool in different directions. And taking walks in the fields and woods in the changing seasons, changing weather.

Summer green engulfs everything. I can usually see the white of the cottage wall through branches as I walk back from the stream; now it is out of sight behind the laburnum. Four ancient privies hidden away in the network of gardens – long disused, but officially Grade II listed – are even more obscured by their lush foliage. The wooden doors are padlocked, traces of paint, pink and blue. You have to stoop and push branches aside to see them. But why would you? They're left over from who knows when, strange survivors into a world of all mod cons. Elsewhere lawnmowers hum, tidying small and proud plots of ground.

Once I arrived at Cambridge things were altogether more purposeful. Not that many of us had careers planned ahead. Certainly many of us in the humanities were there for the sheer pleasure of study for its own sake. Few of us made any plans until our final year, and even then the options were always vague: teaching, publishing, the BBC, the Civil Service, advertising . . . something would turn up. For women, the opportunity to try our skills in university activities was strictly limited. Women could not be members of the Union, or of the Footlights: careers in politics and show business that would open up for the next generation were harder for us. The university's magazines were virtually a male monopoly. The careers advice system was little more than an amiable woman sitting behind a big desk in a large house along a leafy lane on the outskirts of town. I came away with a handful of leaflets for companies that didn't interest me. I don't remember even reading them. There seemed no urgency about such things. Nor should there be. Young people have their lives ahead of them: they need time to drift and wander, to try things out, to disappoint and be disappointed. It's the sort of advice I try to pass on to grandchildren.

But it was easier in the 1950s. There were plenty of jobs and no inflation. Wages were steady, prices and rents reasonable. There must have been some of my contemporaries keen for wealth and worldly success . . . but that wasn't how we approached life. Of course we were ambitious. We cared about our reputations, but in our own terms. We wanted to spend our years in fulfilling activity, however we individually defined it. Peter Hall wanted to continue directing plays; Jonathan Miller would become a doctor and man of the theatre; Leslie Bricusse would write musicals; Frederic Raphael would write novels; Mark Boxer would edit magazines. I wasn't sure what I would do. Of course there was always the BBC.

I came down from Cambridge with a traineeship to be a BBC studio manager. It wasn't something for which I was suited, being all about sound waves, cross-plugging and microphone flutter, but it was a toe in the door. Being in London taught me several things that would sway my future choices. They concerned the routines of daily life rather than any search for self-fulfilment. Suddenly the easy-going, unscheduled life of a student was gone. And I was haunted by images of dystopia that warned of what might be to come. T. S. Eliot's *The Waste Land* came menacingly to mind:

> A crowd flowed over London Bridge, so many,
> I had not thought death had undone so many.
> Sighs, short and infrequent, were exhaled,
> And each man fixed his eyes before his feet.
> Flowed up the hill and down King William Street,

To where Saint Mary Woolnoth kept the hours
With a dead sound on the final stroke of nine.

I saw this as a destiny to be avoided at any cost. Somehow I overlooked the fact that Eliot himself had worked in a city bank for eight years. I had also seen Fritz Lang's *Metropolis*, a lavish film set in a future where wealthy industrialists and their idle children lord it over oppressed masses living in the depths of misery. (It was set in 2026!) Here was I travelling on the crowd-packed Underground twice a day at rush hour. Unless something changed I seemed destined to be doing this for the next forty years. I felt myself on the way to becoming just such an Eliot/Lang wage slave. There and then I made a decision I have kept to ever since: I would seek a working life of irregular hours and unpredictable routine.

It's called being a freelance. And it set me free.

The secret of a happy freelance life is to round up as many offers as you can and then choose the ones you like best. Certainly in the early years this requires enormous amounts of persistence and willpower, and keen attention to how others are managing their lives. I had noticed when I was working as a radio studio manager at Broadcasting House that I would sometimes preside over the control desk and see a sequence of individuals each arrive with a script, have some minutes' consultation with a producer then read the script into the microphone, repeat where there had been fluffs and depart with the prospect of a cheque for three pounds in the post. Each of them had a tale to tell, some modest expertise that would provide an item within a magazine programme. It might be *Woman's Hour*, or *London*

Fritz Lang's Metropolis, *1927*

Tonight. I noticed, and thought to myself, hmm, I could do that!

I couldn't, of course. I had no expertise. As a trained studio manager I knew enough to go out into the world with an Uher tape recorder and use it correctly. So the next thing was to find out what radio producers were looking for. In those days the *Radio Times* provided the names of the producers for every programme. I went through several copies with a fine-tooth comb.

I listed all those producers whose radio programmes appealed to me and wrote to each of them. It was a substantial list. Surely it would bear fruit. Only a few failed to reply at all. Of the rest, more than half turned me down outright. Those that remained had the kindness to let me down gently, saying they had no need in the immediate future. But it was the glimmer of hope I needed. I kept their letters and threw

the rest away. Three months later I wrote again. A couple
asked me to come and see them. I was inching nearer.

My first transmitted radio broadcast was an interview on
the London local news telling how a pigeon fancier in south
London was angering his neighbour by the extent and noise
of his pigeon coops. I made my approaches and arrived at the
family home. I inspected the coops in the garden and then we
sat down and I invited the man to talk. And talk. And talk.
I felt fine about that, thinking I must have a knack of getting

In the offices of McCann Erickson: I struggle to become a copywriter

people to open up. I returned with the brown tape wound on a
spool – that's how we did it in those days. When the producer
saw it he groaned. The item was due to run two and a half minutes at the most. I had recorded a good twenty. He sent me off
to supervise the editing. The editor was no kinder: he sat there
and unwound the tape, letting the brown tape puddle into a
heap on the cutting-room floor, yards and yards of it. What

was he meant to do with this? In the end it was re-wound and I was packed off into a room on my own to listen through, select the meatier parts of the interview and indicate what he could discard. Today reporters make their own items from start to finish, writing and recording their commentary and delivering the piece ready for transmission. In the 1950s the equipment was more cumbersome. And so was I. Today no one would have given me a second chance. But in the event, my piece was not inept and I would be invited back . . . but not immediately.

Meanwhile things were happening in television. The new Television Centre over in West London was recently opened and the BBC was recruiting. I got myself on some sort of rota auditioning for interviewers. I didn't pass. I have never passed any audition. But I watched the others who were auditioning before and after me. I noted what I thought they did well and what they did wrong. And then I had a stroke of luck. One of the auditionees was working as a researcher on a television programme in the Midlands, where they too were looking for new talent. He offered me a three-minute spot on his programme. I grabbed the chance and it was there, on a local programme for Associated Television, that I put what I'd learned from the others into practice. It must have worked.

This purposeful opportunism was to serve me well in the decades ahead. I talked my way into jobs that didn't yet exist. In the early 1980s I persuaded Brian Wenham, the new head of BBC 2, that what the new programme he had just launched – *Newsnight* – really needed was an arts correspond-ent. At that time television current affairs programmes simply didn't consider reporting the arts. That was left to magazine programmes and possibly – if a famous actor had died, or

Prince Charles had exhibited some watercolours – a mention on the news. But Brian and the editor, George Carey, went for it, and I was to enjoy some seven years delivering two or three film reports a week. I was also drafted onto its rota of co-presenters. Early in its existence *Newsnight* had two presenters; the auxiliary one who read the news and introduced minor items was usually a woman. Jenni Murray – later the doyenne of *Woman's Hour* – and I both took our turns. We knew our place. Soon we were being ruefully referred to as 'the programme wives'.

I made it this far because throughout the 1960s and early 1970s I had been one of the presenters of *Late Night Line-Up*. It was my biggest challenge, and in professional terms the making of me. *Line-Up*'s remit was to discuss television itself. BBC 2 had only just launched and television held its audiences in thrall in a way that doesn't happen now. There were no video recorders in those days so the entire audience sat down to watch the same programmes at the same times. Entire families committed their evenings to watching whatever was on. Comedy shows and soap operas often had audiences of more than ten million; some could tip twenty million. So there was plenty of meat for *Line-Up* to get its teeth into. And I was one of four presenters in the studio, live at least three and sometimes four times a week. We didn't have huge audiences ourselves, of course, but the daily presence of the programme, its lively range of talk, jazz, pop and nonsense, brought it and me a considerable profile. It also brought a problem.

I was by the mid-1960s juggling the mix of marriage, young children and my enthusiasm for interesting work. I was keen on all three. I had accepted, as part of how things were, that I would be primarily asked to work on what were then considered women's programmes: I had cut my teeth on an afternoon talk show called *Home at 4.30*, and on a Sunday teatime programme for young people called *Meeting Point*. It wasn't the hard-nosed journalism of current affairs or news, which remained exclusively the territory of men. But the new wave of feminism was stirring, was making itself heard, albeit it in a 'mind-if-I-join-the-boys' kind of way. I had dared to knock on the door of the BBC's Head of News, a droll drinker called Derek Amoore, and ask what plans he had to allow a woman to read the news. He had none. And never would have. He made that clear. Now, would I like a drink?

This wasn't in any way a personal disappointment because it wasn't a job I wanted for myself. Rather, I wanted it as a stride forward for the role of women. What I didn't reckon with was a sideswipe that came from left-field: a well-meant piece of gallantry, but which locked me out of serious consideration for more weighty programmes for a decade. In a *Radio Times* article the humourist and comedy writer Frank Muir dubbed me 'the thinking man's crumpet'.

In today's terms we would speak of the phrase 'going viral'. In no time at all I was called that by every tabloid in Fleet Street, and even the broadsheets felt they had to refer, almost apologetically, to the fact I had been so described. Without any intention or contribution on my part I had been defined and labelled in a way I could not defy or escape. I had lost control – in publicity terms at least – of who I was.

———

I break my thoughts and take a walk in the sun, shaking off old regrets, the road not taken. The summer skies darken. Over beyond the hill the clouds are low. The hill is wooded, its trees thick with undergrowth. Seen from a distance it offers a clear outline on the horizon: I use it to get my bearings. But walking there makes me stumble and lose my sense of direction. Now its silhouette is blurring as the rain covers the slopes. I am still in dry fields, but watching the downpour head towards me. The leaves and grasses rattle under the impact. The rain enfolds me, closing in. I hug my arms round me in a narrowing world. My shoes squelch in the mud. I plod forward. Then it passes . . . the hedges emerge, listening. I see the hill again and head for home and a place to be dry.

———

At *Newsnight* in the 1980s I was thrown into an even greater drama. I was sacked from the programme. In 1987 John Birt arrived at the BBC as Deputy Director-General and set about turning the place upside down. He, an admirer of McKinsey, was all set to introduce market forces into the arena of programme-making. He called a meeting in the largest studio and summoned all the news and current affairs fraternity. Charles Wheeler, the brilliant foreign correspondent, who was the only one still to use shorthand, took down Birt's speech verbatim. Someone else secretly filmed it – I have a bootleg copy to this day. Birt enlarged on the need to give the public more understanding of current affairs; he spoke of setting up specialist units, of major reorganisation. He never spoke of the arts. I was to discover my job was summarily abolished, arts reporting abandoned and me discarded. The BBC did this without any thanks for what I had contributed to the programme and with a callousness as to what it would mean to me personally. No one called me into an office, or had a quiet but apologetic word, and it was left to friends to organise a modest leaving party. Nothing. No one in the programme hierarchy spoke to me about it at all. It was my agent they told, ringing him with the news that my contract would not be renewed. (I learn they haven't changed their ways, recently meting out the same treatment to the singer Tom Jones when he was dropped from *The Voice*.) I was shell-shocked. I had been in steady though freelance employment for some six years and had grown used to a job I loved and did well. Now I was out on my own again. It was a hard lesson well learned.

I didn't have to wait long. Out of the blue came an invitation that was to be a renewal of my association with the Religious Department of the BBC. I was invited by its producer Olga Edridge to present *Heart of the Matter*, which, in three series of six programmes each year, tackled the moral issues raised by current events. This was quite a serious move. I was leaving the world of creativity and entertainment, a place of inspiration and expression, but also of risky finances and famous artists, for a place where we would be weighing up human values, the conflicting duties of public life and the moral issues of the day: I was soon deep into questions surrounding GM foods, sex education in schools, female genital mutilation. I travelled abroad to meet Israeli peacenik soldiers who were refusing conscription; the East German pastors whose churches made the first moves towards the fall of the Berlin Wall; the children of 'the disappeared' murdered in Argentina's Dirty War. I corresponded with Myra Hindley who was hoping for parole and I won the first long interview for British television with Nelson Mandela on his release from Robben Island. It was a thoroughly engrossing job and I was completely absorbed by it. But the Birt revolution was continuing. *Heart* was put out to an independent company where it continued to thrive. Then its budgets were cut and the format confined to little more than studio discussion. Its scheduled time was moved to a later hour: audiences fell. Soon the BBC decided to end it all together. I have no idea why. Certainly there has been no successor programme where the moral searchlight is shone on current world events. Perhaps there should be: the need seems greater than ever. But by this time I had learned not to be distressed by events I couldn't control. Nor to expect loyalty from the BBC. I just had to keep on going.

A successful freelance needs many options, and if they don't come your way then make them happen for yourself. From

Me with Mandela

my early 1960s days I had been offering up suggestions for programme formats to different BBC departments. I had some success. David Attenborough, as Controller of BBC 2, let me make a pilot for a series called *The Scholars*. I was aware that a generation of scholars whose contributions to academia had been outstanding was now growing older. I wanted to catch them for television before it was too late. For the pilot we chose to profile the classicist, bon viveur and Warden of Wadham College, Oxford, Maurice Bowra. I spent a delightful day in his company. He spoke of bitter memories of the First World War, his love of the classics and his vigorous views on education. I remember his rather shy kindness. When he explained that he always had a nap after lunch, I said I would do the same. He fetched a rug and almost tenderly wrapped it round me as I lay on his sofa. The pilot for *The Scholars* led nowhere; no series followed. But somewhere in the BBC Archive is this long-forgotten record of someone mentioned high and low in memoirs of his day, admired and adored by his peers and generations of students. I shall be sad if it has vanished.

Along the way I have made other sorties in the broadcasting world. I wrote and had produced four radio plays, initiated a series called *Generation to Generation*, and submitted a lively format called *Chain Reaction* . . . which was refused. But someone else must have had the idea too, because it's currently running on Radio 4. Perhaps the initiative I am most proud of happened back in 1977, when the tide of feminism was running strong. I persuaded Granada Television to let me chair a series called *Pandora's Box*: six half-hour discussions about justice, education, health, etc. There was one component of the format that made it unique then, and unique now. All those on the panels were women. No men were invited or involved. And what's more, we never referred to the fact. We decided there would be no 'Oh, look, women can do this too!' It would simply be an accepted fact that we could. Not bad for the 1970s! When there was a media flurry, in summer 2015, around the fact that Laura Keunssberg interviewed three women on *Newsnight* I sighed a sigh. Some of us spearheaded this sort of thing decades ago. Did no one notice?

Life has rolled forward, bringing me just the right opportunities to fill my days with the two things that matter most to me: ideas and personal encounters. I have chaired a revival of *The Brains Trust*, made a television series about my generation . . . called *My Generation*, caused a frisson of scandal with a series called *Taboo*, explored how and why people think what they do in a series called *Belief*, and gone *Inside the Ethics Committee* to examine the finer points of medical ethics. Currently Sky Arts have me as a co-presenter with Frank Skinner of their annual search for the Sky Arts Artist of the Year. All this has fed my mind and my imagination, and brought me colleagues who have often become friends.

I expected things to get more difficult as I got older. So I took avoiding action. As my seventieth birthday approached I contacted Alan Rusbridger, the then editor of the *Guardian*, with another of my self-invented schemes. Would his paper like a column written by someone of seventy chronicling what it is to grow old in contemporary Britain? I cited the increase in the number of older people, the scope for more satisfying and diverse lives, the problems around issues of health, transport, housing. The new column was called 'Just Seventy', in an echo of a magazine I hadn't heard of, called *Just Seventeen*. I was thrilled to be writing regularly and when that column exhausted itself I wrote subsequently for the *Independent* and *The Times*. I am now regularly on the comment pages of the *Daily Telegraph*.

One move often promotes another. It must have been my articles about the old that in 2008 caused Harriet Harman to invite me to become the government's spokesperson for older people. The Labour government was pushing through the Equality Bill and they wanted me to bring attention to changes to retirement, pension, social care and employment law. I visited many organisations responsible for the welfare of the old, I handed out awards to deserving carers, I made speeches about part-time working and late-life learning, and wrote to local councils, MPs and Citizens' Advice Bureaux when people brought their particular problems to my attention. But it wasn't easy: I found it depressing that I couldn't solve the intractable problems that our bureaucratic and convoluted way of life throws up. Then the experience brought another unexpected initiative. Ed Miliband asked me to become a working Labour peer in the House of Lords. I was seventy-nine years old and it was likely to be my last job offer. I accepted.

The House of Lords includes many different sorts of people – the hereditaries, the bishops, party donors, former MPs and ministers . . . and many who turn up to help along what it is that the Lords actually do: scrutinise and improve the legislation sent through from the Commons. That is what I do there, keeping an eye on laws that concern the old, medical ethics, education (I am also President of Birkbeck, University of London) and the arts. In coming years the Lords will be drastically reformed. It certainly needs it. Until then, while there is work to be done I shall continue to attend.

The future of work may well be more like my own unpredictable course than the routine nine to five job for life of the post-war decades. Recent shifts to low-wage, zero-hours contract employment suggest it might go that way. Individuals will need to maximise the benefits: freedom to try out different ways of life, plenty of variety, a greater range of colleagues, the deployment of different skills. But it's a precarious life. If working patterns become less predictable, society will need to provide new ways of paying mortgages, building up pensions, organising family life and integrating communities. The workforce will need to be adaptable, confident and willing to go on acquiring new skills. But that will be for future generations to sort out.

On Love

Once Adam and Eve were expelled from the Garden of Eden we knew we were in trouble. Ever since they left Paradise we have struggled to get the matter of sex and love sorted out. All the religions of the world model their mythology on human behaviour: the Bible tells of lots of begetting and admired leaders such as Abraham and King David taking concubines and confusing the matter of inheritance and power. Abraham's wife Sarah, being too old to conceive, offered him her maid Hagar instead, by whom he had Ishmael, the first surrogate baby. When Sarah surprisingly conceived at a great age and bore Isaac, Abraham expelled Ishmael and Hagar to the desert, where they became the ancestors of the Ishmaelites.

We live with the children of Isaac and of Ishmael to this day: Jews, Christians, Muslims. Rome and Greece were if anything worse, having gods who, despite having goddess wives, went frolicking among maidens and nymphs disguised as bulls, swans and the odd shower of gold. The tradition survives: showers of gold still have the power to seduce in our own time. Meanwhile the goddess wives were furious and took various forms of revenge . . . Don't ever let them tell you things were better in the olden days.

Religions set up their own rules and enforced them with different degrees of rigour. Jesus stopped the stoning of women for adultery but the practice survives in the Arab world. And whoever decided that their religion required a celibate male priesthood couldn't have known the trouble they were storing up for centuries to come. Dietary laws and fasting – Lent, Ramadan – feature in many religious practices, intended as an exercise in self-discipline, but today often taken as a chance to lose weight and give the liver a rest. In Burma many young children are signed up as Buddhist monks for a given period of time. They have their hair shaved and wear the appropriate robes: saffron for boys, and, I'm sorry to say, pink for girls; both genders study meditation.

Most religious traditions began long ago and it must be significant that they have lasted and evolved over time. Their very endurance suggests some inner strength that appeals to the human psyche. More recent systems of belief – Scientology, say, or Christian Science – owe their origins to strong personalities, L. Ron Hubbard and Mary Baker Eddy, who had the confidence and authority to impose their world-view on others. It must be the case that Moses, Mohammed, Jesus and Paul were outstandingly powerful individuals with the will and drive to convince others to follow them. At the heart of their message each preached the love of God and love of one's fellow man, the enduring moral directive of religious teaching. But alongside these abstract directives the human race has continued grappling with the more earthy matter of personal love, its vagaries and the power of sex to bond and to disrupt human behaviour. And so it goes on . . . but some of it changes.

The evolution of sex and love has brought mankind great misery and great poetry. Today we live in a world of mixed and interlocking cultures: some still wrap women up and hide them away, some still cut bits off their newborn children – girls and boys – and the supposedly sophisticated West goes in for semi-nudity, serial marriages and heavy doses of therapy. Every generation somehow comes to believe its own mores are not only desirable but the way things should be. My life has spanned different outlooks on love and sex: post-Victorian morality, the indulgence of the bright young things, the sexual intensity of the post-war romantics, the 1960s freedoms of the pill, the emerging tolerance of the 1990s towards today's pick and mix options that embrace gay marriage, surrogacy, IVF, conception beyond the menopause and, more recently, the prospect of eliminating diseases and abnormalities by manipulating our genes. Alongside these varieties of love and sex come things that aren't so welcome: domestic violence, pornography, child abuse . . . and the disclosures and disapproval of what went on in the past. From the vantage point of age I view a landscape of ever-shifting values and customs. There is just one absolute: the human need for love.

We had been reading John Donne, I remember. It wasn't a set text. Our English teacher at our well-mannered girls' grammar school would have blushed to confront giggling teenage girls with his more explicit love poems. So we must have sought them out for ourselves and shared them privately, one to one, much as the boys at the boys' grammar were doing with the magazine *Lilliput*. It came as a shock, a warm, comforting shock, to know that a long-dead and famous poet wrote about the sort of things we were beginning to know. 'I am two fools, I know / For loving, and for saying so'. Then one of us shared it with her boyfriend. It bonded them even closer. There may well have been a run on the bookshop. There was only one in Stockport at the time, down by the bridge Lowry painted and opposite the Carlton cinema. 'License my roving hands and let them go; / Before, behind, between, above, below.' Suddenly the gang I hung out with began whispering lines of poetry to each other and smiling.

Don't misunderstand: there was so far no overt sexual behaviour going on among us. We were all virgins and innocent. But eager too. Then one evening, walking home with Vivienne from a dance, Robin made his move. The walk home took a long time and involved significant pauses under trees and beside mossy walls. The next day Vivienne took a piece of classroom chalk and traced the path they had taken, pausing to mark the pavement with a large cross at each stopping point. We went to see: there were six. Six stopping points, each hallowed by the spirit of John Donne, 'Oh, my America! my new-found-land' . . . except that this was Stockport where it rains a lot and the crosses were soon gone.

I don't know when I stopped having crushes on girls and started to have them on boys. The former usually involved – in the John Donne tradition – the exchange of poems about the nature of God, love and loyalty. I was trying to make sense of all three at the time and felt they must be connected. Pop songs of the day made rather soupy reference to yearnings and delayed gratification: Frank Sinatra begging for five minutes more continues, 'All week long I dreamed about our Saturday date / Don't you know that Sunday morning you can sleep late?' – hardly a come-on for today's young lovers. For our part, we were indeed innocent and compliant with our parents' morality. Change was to come slowly.

I was the subject of crushes too and learned that the kind response was to sign autographs and pose occasionally for a photograph. This was what counted as total consummation. They were harmless times. And yet looking back I can see there was something valuable about this emotional apprenticeship. This brief period of time when we checked out how we felt about ourselves, tested our own emotions against each other, no harm done. It seems now to have been a useful interim between close but fraught family bonds and the overcharged sexual intensity that was to come.

I don't know whether the world today gives space for the dawning of intimacy. What I know of the young is from observing them and from reading about them. They seem a whole lot more spontaneous and uninhibited than we were: there is a joyful frankness and an enquiring attitude to life that can only serve them well. They seem comfortable in their own bodies. But they are under pressures such as never came my way; their options are far greater, their opportunities more open. At the same time the world of advertising, consumerism and popular culture surrounds them with images – abundant, garish, thrilling – that must make independent choice hard. Add to that the febrile rumour mill that is social media, the attractions of belonging within a set of group-think friends, the hubbub of educational expectations . . . and I am not entirely surprised by episodes of self-harm, anorexia and depression.

The post-war years were the high days of romantic love for us all. From the nineteenth century writers and poets had charted the territory. Jane Austen's lovers fell for each other while looking out for marriage. Charlotte Brontë created Rochester; Emily conjured Heathcliff. Byron and Shelley fled abroad to escape the notoriety of their free-loving lives. George Eliot wove stories of misjudgement and devotion. Thomas Hardy told of local loyalties and betrayals . . . for all of them the search for truth and beauty was the lodestar. Then came D. H. Lawrence, consumptive son of a Midlands coal miner who, egged on by an ambitious and devoted mother, took the search into feelings deeper than before. Feelings were what mattered; authentic feelings were somehow heroic. They had moral weight. To deny them was to distort our true selves. And for Lawrence, important among these feelings was sex.

Lawrence had a turbulent and persecuted life: his novels were suppressed due to alleged obscenity, his marriage to a German, Frieda, brought him under suspicion of being a spy. His paintings – put on show in London in 1929 – were seized by the police and only released on condition they were never shown in England again. The Lawrences fled the country and took up a travelling life, finally ending their days in Taos, New Mexico, where Lawrence is buried. I was later to visit the shrine to his memory there and recall with some poignancy my early devotion to the ideas in which he believed.

But Lawrence died in 1930, so why were so many of us in the 1950s influenced by his work and his message? His life had not all been persecution; he had his admirers and supporters. On his death E. M. Forster described him as 'the greatest imaginative novelist of our generation'. More significantly for his continuing reputation he was championed by the literary critic F. R. Leavis, whose savage polemics held many Cambridge English students of the 1950s in thrall. Most tellingly for me, Lawrence – in *The Rainbow* and *Women in Love* – grappled with the nature of female need, sexuality and friendship. Here were books that went deep into my own life as the best books can. Although for many his writing – especially *Lady Chatterley's Lover* – was alarmingly explicit, what mattered was the way he struggled to express the swooning and ecstatic nature of sex. Reopening them today I find much of them ponderous and overblown. At the same time I can see why I was drawn to their lyrical intensity:

> Without speaking, he took her hand across, under the wrap, and with his unseeing face lifted to the road, his soul intent, he began with his one hand to unfasten the buttons of her glove, to push back her glove from her hand, carefully laying bare her hand. And the close-working, instinctive subtlety of his fingers upon her hand sent the young girl mad with voluptuous delight.

Will younger generations read Lawrence? I very much doubt it. Most of them would find it repetitive and obsessed: it would have no relevance to their lives. Sex probably isn't like that any more. Lawrence and what he said, and the way he said it, was matched with his time, and that time has gone. But what remains are occasional dazzling sequences of prose, his love of nature and his capacity to isolate and adore the particular moment. For these unique gifts I hope some of those who come later will find the space and time to value him.

The romantic headiness of the post-war years spread further than the novels being written at the time. A royal crisis crystallised the current state of public morality. I had been quite a royal follower as a young teenager, cutting out newspaper pictures of Princess Elizabeth's wedding dress. I had never seen anything as glamorous. By the early 1950s my mood had gone into reverse and I assumed a mood of what I would call 'teenage snide', a mood only intensified by the scandal. In 1953 Group Captain Peter Townsend, the royal equerry who had being wooing the Queen's younger sister Princess Margaret, proposed marriage. The problem was that he was a divorced man. Concern was expressed by all sorts of people who I thought might well have minded their own business. But the fact the Princess was in the line of succession gave them official permission to interfere. The entire Cabinet expressed their view that the marriage was impossible; so did the prime ministers of all the Commonwealth countries; and of course the Church of England turned its full firepower on the hapless pair. Naturally I wanted Princess Margaret to throw over all their advice and give up all for true love. Instead she bottled out, deciding she did not want to give up her royal status and all the flummery that goes with it. She turned down her lover. I sensed she was never truly happy again.

I wasn't alone in willing her to make the bold choice. The public had in numerous polls expressed their approval of the match. The mood was that the country was on the cusp of change. What brings such a shift? Converging in the 1950s were significant circumstances: relief at a war being over; a sense that we now deserved some fun; having more things to buy; burgeoning advertising that promised the good life; the coming of ITV; the proliferation of books, magazines and films; a turning from outward matters – wars, rationing – to more introspective ways of thinking. Sympathy for the lovelorn Princess was one.

Sympathy for Celia Johnson was another. But her story wasn't easy either – this was the era of frustrated passion. In 1945 she starred in the film *Brief Encounter*, which caught exactly the prevailing sexual morality . . . monogamous marriage and the threat to it of an illicit love affair. Celia Johnson trembled on the brink of adultery with Trevor Howard while Rachmaninov thundered on the soundtrack. Audiences were swept away by its passion and intensity; Celia Johnson was nominated for an Oscar; and the film has been referenced since by dramas as diverse as Alan Bennett's *The History Boys* and an episode of the television series *Shameless*. In 1953 *From Here to Eternity* had a similar impact. This time, Deborah Kerr and Burt Lancaster thrashed around in the breaking waves on the shores of Hawaii, an officer's wife having an affair with a sergeant as the war with Japan looms large. Again sexual frustration is at the heart of the tension, a frustration that can't be resolved within the moral parameters of the time. All this was sexy and illicit. It appealed to our romantic natures, but outraged our sense of how things should be.

Then times changed. Gradually the belief spread that people should not be required to live unhappy lives. The taboos on divorce, which always hit women harder, were relaxed. In my teens I had only known one divorced woman and she was spoken of in disapproving whispers. Besides, she peroxided her hair, another sign of a loose woman. Now it was conceded that you should marry for love, and when love faded or failed to mellow into comforting companionship, then people should be allowed a second chance at the same institution. Besides, men were unfaithful and women were seduced; a new honesty opened to scrutiny and gossip what had formerly been covered up.

In 1963 the Profumo affair had everyone boggling at the whiff of sleaze in high places. We were holidaying in Venice as the story broke and rushed to find as many English-language newspapers as we could. The press only slowly let the story out. We were greedy for details. Christine Keeler was revealed as having affairs with both John Profumo, the Secretary of State for War, and with Yevgeny Ivanov, a Soviet naval attaché. The public nature of the scandal came as a shock to Prime Minister Harold Macmillan, who had long since settled into tolerance of his own wife's infidelity (Lady Dorothy had for years been the mistress of Robert Boothby, MP) but that affair never reached the papers. Boothby wrote to his friend the press baron Lord Beaverbrook, 'Don't let your boys hound me.' He was safe. But Profumo lied to the House of Commons, Macmillan resigned and an era was over.

The year 1963 was a landmark date for Philip Larkin

too – the year of his poem 'Annus Mirabilis'. The first verse is famous, but it is the second that captures the bleakness of the 1950s:

> Sexual intercourse began
> In nineteen sixty-three
> (which was rather late for me) –
> Between the end of the Chatterley ban
> And the Beatles' first LP.
>
> Up to then there'd only been
> A sort of bargaining
> A wrangle for the ring,
> A shame that started at sixteen
> And spread to everything.

I have had two long marriages in my life. Each has been extremely important to me; each was born of its time and lived out its length through the stages of passion, commitment, contentment, ending eventually and with sadness in estrangement and divorce. Intimacy is a private matter and doesn't find its place comfortably in a survey of my times. Only this: I see marriage as the boldest and most honest attempt two people can make to know each other fully over time. They can do this under the aegis of religion or not, regardless of gender, ethnicity, class or career. It is within marriage that we grow to express our deepest selves, share trust and honesty, tenderness and passion, survive disagreements and disloyalty.

Yet we also become dependent, sharing creatures

surrendering something of ourselves into a common unity. In my experience marriage sucks you into the orbit of the other, sometimes with too great a power. The needs of each become mutually dependent; autonomy goes out of the window. People speak of making allowances, compromising, finding an acceptable middle way. Many tell me they have achieved it. But I often wonder at what cost. Those who find this elusive balance are happy indeed. It is a fine and delicate equation. But when work or physical absence, other attachments or diverging lifestyles intervene the dependence comes under stress. Sometimes it is torn apart.

I have spent over half my living years within such relationships. I cannot imagine my life without having done so. I am the mother of two children and the grandmother of six. My bonds with them now sit at the heart of who I think I am. I have lived through early estrangements from my own parents and been through tough times when my children were in their teens. We have not always seen eye to eye; they have made determined efforts to strike out on their own and decide their own identities. Families are not sanctuaries of conformity and acquiescence.

But over the years I have grown to recognise their importance. We, after all, have no choice in the matter. It is what knits us together. Being a link in the generations is humanity's challenge to the dark, the bulwark against time and change. We may like or not like each other, we can stay close or drift apart. We can holiday together, meet up occasionally or do no more than send Christmas cards. But that unchosen network of connections and genes holds us, benignly for the most part, at the centre of our own lives. I consider myself very lucky.

In my later years I have firm bonds with my closest family; warm bonds with the next ripple out from the centre; and I am in touch with those on the outer edges whom I have not met for decades.

The very unpredictability and unavoidability of what family members make of their lives sets their network apart from those we have chosen – friends, acquaintances and colleagues. To be part of a family is to be part of life and its unavoidable patterns. It fixes us in space and time; it defines where we belong. And it never ceases to exist.

Today's views of love and sex are rooted in the 1960s. Again a convergence of influences, medical and social, made change even faster. The availability of the pill meant women could enjoy sex without fear of pregnancy. I had married in the 1950s and been refused birth control advice by an Irish Catholic doctor; the search to get what I needed had been humiliating. I welcomed the pill as a revolution for women. It wasn't the only one. Moves towards more women taking paid work, and the spread of feminist ideas and texts, shifted the power balance. Publishing seized the day. In 1972 Alex Comfort's *The Joy of Sex: A Gourmet Guide* sold twelve million copies worldwide. It depicted in line drawings a vast range of sexual positions for a man and a woman: he with a straggly beard, she with hairy armpits and stringy hair. It was all designed to be informal and casual. In fact, they were husband and wife. Homosexual sex was not mentioned.

There was also a move to include teenagers. I still have my copy of *The Little Red School Book*, a title echoing Mao's *Little Red Book* of Cultural Revolution China. It was written and published in Denmark, translated into English in 1971 and set out straightforward facts about two issues: sex and school. It urged children to rebel against their elders . . . but in the nicest possible way. 'Porn is a harmless pleasure . . . Anyone who mistakes it for reality will be greatly disappointed.' 'Is pot dangerous? There's no definite answer to this yet.' 'Don't accept marks as the be all and end all.' The publishers also recommended the speeches of Castro and essays of Che Guevara.

in 1970 the magazine *OZ* had been handed over to a group of schoolchildren to edit; they came up with a rude parody of the *Daily Express*'s much-loved Rupert Bear comic strip, using Robert Crumb cartoons. In the subsequent obscenity trial the magazine's editors were defended by John Mortimer, later the creator of *Rumpole of the Bailey*, and Geoffrey Robertson, who would become one of the country's leading human rights barristers. *Late Night Line-Up* sent me along to report on the trial; we were hopelessly biased in favour of the accused. Their defence took on the high-minded tone of moral superiority: 'the case stands at the crossroads of our liberty, at the boundaries of our freedom to think and draw and write what we please'. The language is not unfamiliar in today's debates about *Charlie Hebdo* and Danish cartoons. The three accused were found guilty of conspiracy to corrupt public morals, taken briefly to prison and then released on appeal. What outraged us most was that the prison authorities cut off their fashionable flowing locks. Short hair was associated with criminals and soldiers, and distinctly old-fashioned.

From the 1960s onwards almost everything between the sexes could be spoken of and illustrated.

The world of explicit advice, details of intimacy, confessions of personal pain and inadequacy has extended and expanded. And goes on expanding. *Late Night Line-Up* also sent me on a trip to an Amsterdam television studio (we were invited to show them how such a programme as ours could work for them) and we took time out to buy sex handbooks openly on sale in shops. The Dutch had always been more explicit in the public discourse about sex, and less guilty or embarrassed. I would return to Amsterdam in the 1990s to make a programme about a sex factory . . . girls signing on to work a full day displaying themselves for all-round cameras in numerous porn poses and responding to credit-card callers from all over the world asking for specific favours. They worked in a factory unit, arriving daily, parking their cars and paying their taxes. The business was registered in the Dutch economy.

But within the sexual revolution there was another story.

In February 1988 I began to receive letters from all over the country, from Anglicans, Methodists and Baptists. I had put myself on their grapevine, so I was not surprised by their arrival. The letter-writers all had three things in common: they were all ministers of Christian churches, they all asked me to keep their secret, and they were all gay. The practice that disqualified them from the ministry – active homosexuality – has been legal in this country since 1967. So *Heart of the Matter* embarked on a programme that asked whether homosexuality was a sin which the Church of England could not tolerate within its clergy, or whether it was a human condition created by God, the equivalent of heterosexuality.

The gay clergy who, speculation said, could constitute up to a quarter of the Church of England priesthood, believed homosexuality to be an orientation, and part of God's created world. Traditionalists believed it to be a sin and a perversion, citing Leviticus and several letters of St Paul, but not mentioning the gospels or Jesus himself, who said nothing on the matter. The Church hierarchy, in trying to hold together such diametrically opposing views, found itself jostled around somewhere between the two, struggling to find a form of words that would keep everyone happy.

In November 1987 the General Synod had debated a Private Member's Motion that declared 'fornication, adultery and homosexual acts to be sinful in all circumstances'. It was brought by the Reverend Tony Higton, a vigorous evangelical of intransigently traditional views, which brought him, in Mrs Thatcher's day, invitations to 10 Downing Street. Higton was not at one with the bishops.

The bishops responded to his motion by proposing an amendment. They were keen to tone down the absolutism of his language. But in so doing, so they gave birth to a phrase of distasteful ambiguity that in the event pleased no one: 'homosexual genital acts', they ruled, 'fall short of [the] ideal'. The amendment won a massive majority.

Three months later, in February 1988, the Reverend Jeremy Younger went into the pulpit of St Mary-le-Bow and explained to his congregation why he was leaving the ministry after eighteen years. His parishioners had not been in on the secret of his personal life as an active homosexual, although his partner had shared the vicarage for six years.

On *Heart of the Matter* Jeremy spoke openly, without any of television's proffered disguises: the head in shadow, the distorted voice or the actor playing out the interview. For him the deception was over; the fear had lifted. But then he had already ceased being an officiating minister.

At the end of our programme the Bishop of Chester gave an unwitting clue as to what might occasion our next programme: 'In some ways it's better to be secret about it, I think. It's been the coming out that's caused the problem, hasn't it?'

Almost seven years later, on a Sunday in September 1994, the Right Reverend Michael Turnbull woke to a nightmare. The *News of the World* had headlined the fact that twenty-six years before, at the age of thirty-two, he had committed an act of gross indecency with another man in a public toilet. Now he was about to be installed as Bishop of Durham, the fourth most senior post in the Church's hierarchy. The news threw the media and the Church into turmoil. *Heart of the Matter* went to Durham at the time of the enthronement to ask whether there was hypocrisy at the heart of the Church.

We found that, in the six years since our 1988 programme, attitudes had begun to change. First, the bishops had had a stab at solving the problem. In December 1991 they published a statement, *Issues in Human Sexuality*, forty-eight pages of closely argued text 'which we do not pretend to be the last word on the subject'. Clearly this was not an outright condemnation.

For their part the homosexual clergy had become more confident, more forthcoming, and some of them were angry. The Reverend Niall Johnston was ordained in 1992, and by 1994 was running a support group for gay clergy that had some four hundred members. He had served in the army for ten years, rising to the rank of major and serving in both Northern Ireland and the Falklands. While in the army he had had a nine-year relationship with a soldier he had met at Sandhurst. They had been together – defying army rules against homosexuality – until a car crash in 1990 killed his partner. Niall now spoke openly on our programme, defying the Church to sack him:

> I think that if one had been particularly blatant in the Army, then almost certainly one would have been discharged. But those who knew took the view that it was more important that I was efficient at the job I was doing. They colluded in exactly the same way as the Church is doing today.

The bishops' statement of 1991 that 'homosexual genital acts fall short of [the] ideal' had, in the event, landed the Church with a two-tier approach to homosexuality: practising homosexuality was in reality denied to clergy but permitted to laity.

The double standard was unacceptable to both wings of the argument. Niall found it 'philosophically impossible to justify'. Tony Higton, with his insistence that a proper discipline be applied within the Church, found the two-tier morality a 'diabolical hypocrisy'.

That was as recently as 1995 . . . twenty years ago. By 2015 the law permitting gay marriage was finally passing through the House of Lords. Waheed Alli, a gay Muslim life peer, sprang a subversively dramatic surprise: on the day the Bill was to get its final approval and become the law of the land he arranged that large baskets of pink carnation buttonholes be placed at the doors of the chamber. Each of us who supported the Bill – on both sides of the House, and among the crossbenchers – took one and wore it. There were pleased smiles all round. Helena Kennedy whispered to me, 'This is changing history.' About time.

Betrayal

For eight years in the 1960s I was having an affair with Harold Pinter. He was at the start of a blossoming career and it was *The Caretaker*, first produced at the Arts Theatre in 1960, that was the breakthrough: it made his reputation and set the course for future plays and productions that would make him famous as a writer of outstanding brilliance and a peculiarly original vision. He stood at the threshold of that career.

I was a married woman with a small daughter and a radio producer husband whose work brought us regularly into contact with Harold and his actress wife Vivien. We were both conventional spouses who had married for love and were devoted to our young families; we each lived in rented flats, in Chiswick and Camden, hoping some time soon to buy houses of our own. We shared the common aspirations of our generation to get on in the world. We socialised easily with people like ourselves, upbeat and optimistic about our lives and our futures. So what happened?

Harold was to tell our story in his play *Betrayal*, written in 1978, long after our love affair was over and we were steadily and happily settled, I within my second marriage, Harold with Lady Antonia Fraser, whom he would marry in 1980. Our affair had ended but our friendship had not. Indeed, it could be said to have got stronger over the years. We no longer had the shared flat we had made our home, but we met regularly to tell each other what was happening in our lives, both personal and professional. We both had confidence that it was a strong friendship that would endure. And so it proved. I told Harold how I had met a younger man, an actor/writer who I would go on to marry, my doubts about his age, my concerns about his career. He told me in 1975 how he and Lady Antonia Fraser had come together late one night after the opening of his play *The Birthday Party* at the Shaw Theatre and that something important was happening between them. Later he would ask my advice when Antonia suggested they have a child together. All these confidences were exchanged at a string of restaurants across London, over long and convivial lunches that had all the air of casual encounters. I think for both of us they were more than that.

Then late one afternoon in 1978 a package was hand-delivered to my home. Harold had always dispatched first manuscript copies of each play to a small group of his closest friends. We knew to respond as soon as possible to acknowledge, congratulate and enthuse about the play; given their dazzling quality it wasn't hard to do. Harold, though entirely sure of his own vision, not letting a comma or a pause be challenged, was also deeply needful of support from those he trusted. More than that, he could fly into a wild temper if their response was not forthcoming. I have several notes, written in his large and angry hand, deploring my lack of commitment. But these would come later. For the time being I kept faith with our mutual understanding.

The day the manuscript arrived I was at home alone. My

husband was away. I went to bed early and settled on the pillows to read it through. What I read kept me awake throughout the night. *Betrayal* uses the story of fictional Emma, Jerry and Robert to tell of our falling in love, our subsequent meetings, our second home, the tension of our disloyalty to our partners, and the fact that, unknown to Harold and by a coincidental mix-up of letters, my husband had long since come to know about our affair. This was indeed the case. Together Michael and I had kept this knowledge from Harold, who when the truth eventually emerged was to feel betrayed by my treachery in not telling him what had happened . . . a moral cat's cradle indeed. It makes electrifying theatre. But it made me frantic.

First thing the next morning I was on the phone to Harold and we met later in the day. I was in a great state of distress, somehow reaching out at the possibility that he might make changes. Could he perhaps change the title? I felt the word 'betrayal' seemed particularly targeted at me. I felt a decade's guilt spilling into public view; I felt like one of those women hounded through medieval streets as a witch for having offered healing herbs to a child . . . it's a fanciful parallel, I know, but that's how it felt. The play was surely treacherous, unkind, exposing, ruthless. We discussed the title but, he spelled out, 'the point is there are many betrayals in the play . . . each character has betrayed something or someone . . . every single person'. I was hardly consoled. I was later to learn from his notes for the play that he had considered other titles, among them 'Torcello': the name of the island in the Venetian archipelago the characters visit. I had been there years earlier and strongly urged Harold and Vivien to go, which they had. I would enjoy that as a title: 'Torcello' having nothing but memories of beauty and peace for me. But he refused. He refused even the tiniest changes to the play.

I ran into the indomitable ego of the creative writer. Harold was the only child of doting parents. He was brought up to be exact and fastidious; he expected as much from those around him. If he made a typing error when he was writing his plays he would snatch the sheets from the typewriter, discard them and start again. He could not tolerate a single flaw. He grew to be like that with people. There are accounts of his explosive anger in public places that grew more frequent as he took up political causes. He couldn't bear for things not to be the way he wanted them to be. And in private too: his friends knew to fear and avoid the volcanic temper. On one occasion when he had reduced me to tears in the foyer of the National Theatre, Antonia came with comfort: 'You must know, Joan, it is always with those he loves most that he feels . . . ' I said I understood. But it wasn't easy.

The public unravelling came in 1996. For eighteen years the origins of *Betrayal* had been known to a small circle within the theatre world and among close friends and some family. But even during the media frenzy that occurred when Harold had left Vivien for Antonia the press had not been aware. Vivien was to die believing Antonia was the original of Emma. Then in 1996 Michael Billington published his authorised biography of Harold. Harold had rung me and asked me to collaborate. I was surprised he wanted our story to be told. 'What shall I tell him?' I asked. 'Tell him the truth . . . why not?' And so I did. The biography contained the full background to *Betrayal*, with explanation of how and in what way it reflected our love affair. For a brief period on publication the press went into overdrive, but the story finally fell away and became part of accepted gossip. There was, however, a strange sequel.

In 2003 I published my autobiography. One chapter of it was called 'The Secret', though of course it was no longer any such thing. I thought my account of what lay behind *Betrayal* would add a valuable dimension for Pinter scholars, indeed for anyone who was interested. I told Harold I was doing this, and asked whether I might quote from the play. His letter in reply was terse: it explained how unhappy he was that I was making our relationship public, although he acknowledged, grudgingly, that I was entitled to do so. He went on to refuse my request. The relationship, as I've said, had already been made public seven years earlier by his own biographer. He seemed not to notice.

Then, once *The Centre of the Bed* had been published he renewed his objection, more strongly this time, telling me that he remained very unhappy that I had disclosed his private life to the public. There followed months of estrangement between us.

———

The patterns go on changing: there is no point of arrival. Somehow the giddy excitement that attended losing your virginity, freedom to enjoy your body, learning the mechanics of sex and its athletic variations, all this settled down into what seems a new conformity. Many people in Western societies – gay and straight – now have sex before marriage. Many have children, no longer stigmatised as illegitimate. All indications are that thoughts only turn to marriage when children and mortgages are involved . . . both representing a commitment to something actual and enduring. The varieties of sexual bonds and ways of having children are increasing:

IVF treatment and mitochondrial donation will now make it possible for women with faulty genes to have healthy children; women can have children after the menopause; many gay couples adopt, some get pregnant with sperm either from a stranger or a friend. When the couple are celebrities – Elton John and David Furnish – the story is openly told and widely approved. There is no shame.

The new frontier is in popular culture. It was always the way for young performers to provoke outrage: it is part of their *raison d'être*. Now we have twerking, a bottom-twitching dance which, as performed by Miley Cyrus at the 2013 MTV Video Music Awards, simulated anal sex. The music she was twerking to – Robin Thicke's 'Blurred Lines' – has the lyrics 'So, hit me up when you pass through / I'll give you something big enough to tear your ass in two'. It's hard to know where young performers can go next to explore the limits of what's allowed. Meanwhile swathes of social media have sudden attacks of puritanism. Any Twitter account that insults a woman is swept into a storm about sexual abuse. No one would dare call me the thinking man's crumpet today without getting a severe response from my friend Mary Beard.

Scandal and shame now focus on sexual crimes: violence against and the harassing of women, and sex with children. And often the shock and outrage centre on events long past and only now coming to light. Priests and celebrities have been uncovered as the main offenders over past decades and there is now a sad procession of grey-haired men going to jail.

I write from the heartlands of Western society. It is where I grew up. It is what has shaped me. My experience of how love and sex have shifted in both emphasis and expression is observed from the safety of my middle-class background. The situation in the wider world is vastly different. And throughout recent decades those differences have become increasingly significant for the West. Global reporting and social media make us aware of things that once remained in the shadows. As a woman, what I respond to most and report on are matters that affect the lives of women: forced marriage, female genital mutilation, rape as a weapon of war, rape for its own sake, rules in the name of religion that wrap women in the niqab, the hijab, the chador, the burka. I have met young women who have fled brutal treatment and come to this country seeking asylum. They deserve open arms of welcome in a country such as ours that prides itself on tolerance. They deserve sympathy for their suffering and admiration for their courage. But too often it is not what they get. Many are shut up in the state's detention centres waiting repatriation, often to the very country that was the source of their persecution. Yarl's Wood is a particularly notorious case, with evidence of warders insulting and abusing these vulnerable women. I am part of a campaign to get them better treatment.

So all is not rosy in the move towards freedom and self-fulfilment. And even where I have seen so many improvements – towards tolerance, openness, freedom from fear and inhibition –I wonder how things will change. Here are some ideas that trigger alarm in my mind:

Has feminism with its rightful attention to the details of pay differentials, the continuing burden of childcare, the freedom of sexual display that embraces pornography and the wilder shores of show business ... has all this created a backlash among men?

Are we seeing in violence against women, the brutality of rap lyrics, the move by some religions – Islam in particular – to re-impose more stringent dress codes and rules of behaviour ... all these, in big ways and small, a reaction to the claim by women of a stronger place in world affairs, politics, the workforce and the domestic setting?

Do men feel emasculated, deposed from what earlier cultures saw as their leading role? Has the greatest social change of our time and possibly others' alienated men, who should be its allies?

And what will happen next?

I have seen in my time gay marriage, the acceptance of transsexuals, pregnancies in post-menopausal women – all developments I have welcomed, but which were totally shocking to the world in which I grew up. Where will such progress turn next? Will medicine provide artificial wombs so that pregnancy can be avoided? Will women want that? I sense that societies need to scapegoat the weaker among them. On whom might this burden fall, and how equipped are we to resist it?

I have seen the collapse of traditional marriage as the overriding model of social organisation. I have experienced myself the damage this does to old and familiar structures: I know that children are hurt, even badly traumatised, by their parents' parting. Will this now be the pattern for the future? As if to compensate for this increasing trend, we have made childhood and children the focus of family life, letting their preferences and tastes rule the household, vesting our own self-esteem in how well they do at school, at chess, at football, at giving the best parties. What will happen to children so overindulged when they hit the real world and many of them find they face zero-hours contracts and the minimum wage?

I recognise that older people tend to relish the troubles piling up for the young. We will not be there to see them . . . it is some comfort, but not much. I pour myself a stiff drink to ease the melancholy I've just conjured up.

Every year for the last decade I have received an anonymous St Valentine's Day card. Well, not quite anonymous. A tall grey-haired stranger who claims to have known me as a teenager has approached me at one or two literary festivals. He is very thoughtful and kind. We exchange pleasantries. And then the valentines arrive, sometimes signed. In the year of my eightieth birthday it included these words by R. S. Thomas:

> . . . Take my hand
> A moment in the dance,
> Ignoring its sly pressure,
> The dry rut of age,
> And lead me under the boughs
> Of innocence. Let me smell
> My youth again in your hair.

It was unsigned.

This year there was no valentine.

On Genes

M y sister was irritated.
            'Of course his nose is dripping – he's an old man.
What does he expect?'

'He expects you to put things right for him. Remember
the trouble with the thumb?' My sister's irritation turns into
a long, understanding sigh. She is a nurse and finds people's
preoccupations with minor troubles of minor interest, knowing, as she does, what lies in wait for them. Our father is in
his seventies and we both anticipate the arrival of something
that will in due course carry him off.

We were in our fifties at the time of his complaining; being
in my eighties now I reflect ruefully on whether my own
children are steeling themselves against my inevitable going.
I think they probably are not, given that age itself is a more
robust thing in the twenty-first century.

But back in my father's day . . .

My sister is not unsympathetic, but her irritation stems
from her wanting to help and not being able to. It's what she

brings to their relationship. Father ill, daughter a nurse. It must be a regular pattern.

'Well, loads of old people have dripping noses. Haven't you noticed?' I recall an occasional tramp with a red nose and pendant drip. 'It's what happens as you get older. He'll just have to manage.' And with our sympathy and a ready supply of white handkerchiefs, of which he places a clean one in his sleeve every morning, he carries on and doesn't remark on his infirmity again.

By the time I am his age I too have a dripping nose. Times are different now and I am more assertive than my father in deciding to do something about it. The doctor advises an X-ray. Perhaps my father's generation were more timid of medical paraphernalia, certainly suspicious of X-rays, which had in their early days a reputation for banging large amounts of radiation into the unresisting body. No, even had my sister suggested it – which she of course wouldn't for such a minor irritant – my father would have refused. I do not refuse.

The X-ray shows that the configuration of my sinus passages is such that the bones don't facilitate effective drainage. Clearly I have inherited the same bone structure as my father's nose and thus inherited his drips. But now there is a medical option: I could have a minor operation which basically takes a saw to the bones and widens the drainage channel. I think I have grasped this correctly; I go away with what I can make of the explanation to consider whether to have the operation. I hesitate. I talk to one or two friends about the dilemma: unlike my father, I am not shy of talking about my body and am happy to be frank in ways that my father would have found blush-makingly explicit. But it produces a solution. I have an opera-singer friend who knows all about sinus problems. She tells me about the neti pot, a small pot with a spout that singers, so she tells me, use to keep their sinuses in good order. I go on the internet. My supplier turns out to be running for local office as a Lib Dem. We exchange pleasantries on the matter and then he undertakes to send me a neti pot forthwith. Problem solved. I don't know whether he won or not.

A few years later my son, by now in his mid-forties, mentions that he's due to have some minor operation . . . 'nothing to worry about, but I thought I'd mention it'. Yes, he has inherited the family drip and has already made plans to do something about it. He has scarcely hesitated between the diagnosis and the remedy. The irritatingly narrow bones have passed from generation to generation. What has changed is how differently each generation has dealt with it. My father's resignation has evolved into my son's decision to act.

In the year that follows I discover a grandson has the same problem.

———

I can still see in my mind's eye the lace curtain blowing in the light breeze of the spring day. I see it as I hear my daughter's voice speaking from her hospital bed, the most poignant words in the language: 'Oh, Mum, my boy's not right.' She had given birth an hour or two earlier and it was immediately clear that her son had been damaged in the womb. Our world went crazy.

I don't mean to write here about what that meant and what happened next. Except to tell of the immediate medical response. I was called in to talk to one of the medical team: they wanted to know what each of my parents, grandparents . . . and even further back into the family tree if possible . . . what each had died of. The first generation was easy: my mother of leukaemia at the age of fifty-eight, my father of cancer at the age of eighty-seven. Further back got hazy. I knew my maternal grandmother had died of a brain haemorrhage in her seventies and my grandfather had died in his nineties, simply, I was told, of old age. My paternal grandparents were less clear. I had always understood that my grandmother had died of tuberculosis in her thirties, and my grandfather, an iron turner in a Manchester factory, had died well before her. Their children, orphaned young, never spoke of them except to say the young family had not been able to afford medical treatment. It made them life-long supporters of the welfare state. But it didn't give the medical team the information they needed.

They were looking for some genetic clues as to what might be wrong with my new grandson. But scant records and failed memories were no help. Today things would be different: medical records and family documents are carefully preserved. In future such a medical question would release an avalanche of detail. Longing to help, I felt helpless.

Genetics is now a familiar part of society's medical and family discourse. Its public profile has emerged since the 1970s, but its origins are credited much earlier. In the 1990s I found myself in Brno, second city of the Czech Republic, and in the gardens of the Augustinian abbey there. It was in this very garden that Gregor Mendel had experimented on pea plants, recorded their patterns of inherited qualities and developed the earliest theories of genetics. I was there to make a television programme that would chart the public awareness of genetics in the late twentieth century and the significance for its continuing changes for our moral choices. Not surprisingly Richard Dawkins, whose landmark book *The Selfish Gene* had become a global best-seller back in 1976, was with us.

In the late 1960s I had interviewed James Watson on the publication of *The Double Helix,* his account of the discovery of the structure of DNA which he claimed he had made with his colleague Francis Crick. Subsequent revelations were to accuse him of neglecting the important part played by his colleagues Maurice Wilkins and Rosalind Franklin. In the case of Rosalind, to diminish her role was seen as the outright sexism so characteristic of the times. But I was not to know that when we met. I only knew then that this massive discovery would be shaping our view of human identity and behaviour from then on. I also found James Watson to be a quirky, tense and unpredictable person. Both reactions proved to be accurate.

Throughout the 1990s *Heart of the Matter* would make programmes that charted the use of genetics, as stories began regularly making headlines. We stormed in each week, inviting philosophers, writers, medical authorities, commentators and representatives of religious groups for their points of view. Looking back now, and against the background of current argument, I can trace how attitudes to genetics have been changing over the years.

Heart of the Matter was made within the Religious Department of the BBC. Back when I arrived at the BBC in the 1950s it was a fully-fledged department in its own right, always headed by a Christian cleric, and often staffed by producers with a religious background of their own. There was no question about its remit: it was to make religious programmes including *Songs of Praise*, and report on Church events. I myself did a series of discussions about the meaning of Lent, another about people of strong faith commitments. But as the years went by the secular spirit – including my own – was restless to extend our range. We wanted to talk about world affairs, current events, individual morality. *Heart of the Matter* was born of that spirit, but we were regularly reminded that we worked within a department committed to religious and moral broadcasting. It was the weight of this reminder that sat on my shoulders and probably coloured my commentary of the time. Early this century the department was renamed the Department of Religion and Ethics. In May 2015 the post of Head of Religion and Ethics was axed completely; religion was subsumed, along with science, history and business issues, into a new designation: factual.

Looking back on the early programmes about genetics, they now seem, compared to today's style, overloaded with portentous vocabulary. I spoke of 'human life on earth', 'human destiny', 'playing with the future'. Our graphics featured a naked baby with a rattle (good) and, by contrast, a row of shop-window dummies with expressionless faces lined up in formation (bad). The people I interviewed often referenced Aldous Huxley's novel *Brave New World*; the allegation of 'scientists playing God' was made often. Germaine Greer worried that 'the possibility of one day feeding the world would be at the expense of "the twelve perfumes of rice"'. She maintained that if a gene had survived thus far, then it must be for a reason, and that eliminating it would threaten the gene pool of the human race. Tom Shakespeare, the sociologist who has achondroplasia (in the 1995 programme we referred to him as a dwarf), felt that the notion of perfecting the human race implicit in much of bio-genetics put pressure on disabled people. He and his wife had resisted pressure to abort their achondroplasic daughters. George Steiner was seriously alarmed that we were tampering with 'our coming hence . . . and our going forth', speaking of his fear that tampering with DNA might deprive the world of a Beethoven, a Dostoevsky, a Pascal. This was the discourse that reflected early responses to genetic engineering and its dawning potential.

Slowly the attitude changed. What changed it was events. There was no possibility of stopping the role of genes in our lives. But genetic incidents cropped up that prompted further thought. In 1991 Stephen Mobley had shot and killed a pizza store attendant in Georgia. He was convicted. But on appeal his attorney put forward, by way of mitigating evidence, the defence that he was genetically disposed to seek violent solutions to conflict. The attorney cited recent research that associated a particular gene mutation with violent behaviour in a Dutch family. Researchers analysed Mobley's family tree and found four generations of erratic, violent and abusive behaviour. It wasn't enough. The judge refused permission to have Mobley's DNA tested for the same mutation, saying the scientific evidence of the link was inadequate. Mobley was accordingly sentenced to death and executed. But his became the most widely cited case in which lawyers used genetics in their client's defence.

Research goes on to decide to what extent genetic disorders, mental illness, susceptibility to depression and other personality traits should be taken as mitigating circumstances. I can only think this will become more complex, more argued over and more significant as we try to understand why some people commit crimes and others – often from similar backgrounds – don't.

In parallel, it has been suggested that some genes might also account for thrusting and aggressive drive in the world of business. And how about politics? People with an inherited tendency to violence with their finger on the nuclear button?

In 1990 the case of John Moore finally reached the Supreme Court of California. John told us how in 1976, to treat his hairy-cell leukaemia, his spleen had been removed by Dr David Golde of the UCLA Medical Center. In the following three years Golde's team extracted a cell line from tissue of the discarded spleen and in 1984 obtained a US patent on that very cell line: what John Moore called his own 'genetic essence'. John sued, claiming ownership in the patent which was already yielding commercial value. The Supreme Court rejected his claim, saying that John was not responsible for the invention and an individual could not exercise property rights over discarded tissue.

The same idea surfaced again in 1991 when researchers isolated a cell line from an indigenous tribe in Papua New Guinea whose members carried a gene that predisposes to leukaemia but did not themselves develop the illness. The bid to patent the cell line – unknown to the original tribal members – sparked further controversy. The term 'bio-piracy' began to circulate.

By now there were calls for limits to be set on what could be done. There was a scnsc that as ever-newer uses were being proposed, the technology needed regulation. Louise Brown had been the first baby born by IVF back in 1978, and concerns then had led to an inquiry under the distinguished philosopher Mary Warnock. This led to the UK's Human Fertilisation and Embryology Authority (HFEA) being established by law and coming into being in August 1991. When you have technology plus law it is clear that new procedures are well and truly accepted by society. Since 1978 five million babies worldwide have been born by IVF, for a variety of reasons. One has been the wish to eliminate genetic faults from the family cell line and be sure of having healthy children.

In 1995 *Heart of the Matter* followed the case of Heather Castle, whose brother had died young of muscular dystrophy. She came under the care of Professor Robert Winston, head of IVF at the Hammersmith Hospital. He explained how he had extracted some six to twelve eggs, fertilised as many as possible, then chose two that were free of the defect for Heather's IVF. The programme looked at the broader prospect of not only doing away with disability, but being able to create the kind of child you wanted. We raised the possibility that choosing sex, eye colour, even selecting for sporting or musical skills, might one day be within medical reach. There was media interest when we covered the story of a woman who wanted an abortion because her baby had a cleft palate, a mild condition that can usually be rectified soon after birth.

There was another consequence of all this concern. Bioethics became big business. When I had begun my reporting in the early 1990s there were only one or two hospitals that had thought of setting up ethics committees. Few academics lectured on bioethics; now there are professorships. It is a matter of routine these days, dealing with problems created by the new technology. Enough problems for me to have been presenting a BBC Radio 4 programme – called *Inside the Ethics Committee* – for some eleven years. There is never a shortage of dilemmas.

Almost twenty years on, in February 2015, I find myself sitting alongside Robert Winston in the House of Lords for the debate about the Human Fertilisation and Embryology (Mitochondrial Donation) Regulations 2015 legislation. Mitochondrial donation is the latest technique to be adopted in the field of genetics, and requires acceptance in law for it to proceed further. Mitochondria are present in all human cells; they generate the cells' energy. They have their own DNA which carries just a few genes, but any faults in that DNA can cause serious diseases. The latest proposal is to allow the modification of mitochondrial genes so that women who carry a damaged gene (they are inherited only from our mothers) can bear healthy children. After several consultations and the approval of the HFEA it was finally passing through Parliament.

Opposition to the proposal centred on the fact that it was tampering ever more intrusively with human genes. In its defence, it was explained that this proposed intrusion into the cell nonetheless happens outside the nucleus. It is the nucleus that is critical; it is the nucleus that makes us who we are. And this would not be affected. The debate was intense. It lasted four hours and was full of expert medical and legal opinion. In the course of it Viscount Ridley, an award-winning science writer whose books include *Nature via Nurture*, had this to say:

Is this ethical? We do not, in the twenty-first century, have the luxury of deciding these things in a theological way. If we block an advance of this kind and it turns out it could have eliminated suffering safely, then it is on our consciences in a way that it would not have been thirty years ago, when we could do nothing. In losing our impotence, we also lose our innocence.

The proposal to go ahead was carried by 280 votes to forty-eight.

Ridley identified the essence of the genetics debate. Science is gaining more and more skills in the eradication of conditions judged damaging to the human embryo. PGD (pre-implantation genetic diagnosis), a method of checking out embryos created through IVF, is now applied to more than 250 medical conditions judged undesirable. Scientists are now experimenting with a new method called genome editing. It is not currently allowed in clinical practice because it goes further: it allows for the precise manipulation of genes within the nucleus of any cell. Tony Perry, a molecular embryologist at the University of Bath, suggests that genome editing might one day make possible the elimination of the mutation in the BRCA1 gene and so stop someone inheriting the predisposition to breast cancer. At the moment germline modification is still highly controversial and many scientists are themselves seriously worried that it would be a step too far. There are calls for an international conference on the matter, and for a moratorium on such research.

Clearly we are at the tipping point. Genetics has reached the stage anticipated in our 1995 programme, where science can move from correcting faults in human genes that cause suffering to the ability to create designer babies, made to

measure with chosen hair, eyes, even temperament and apti-
tudes. At which point, what will we have done to free will?

Are we made by nature or nurture? The eternal question
goes on. It is both scientific and philosophical. Medicine is
revealing an increasing number of elements that are inherited:
it has even solved the dripping nose that began this chapter.
But my life has taught me how much both matter. How nature
or nurture prevails in each of us must be a matter for our
own individual temperament, for which we have in the end
to take responsibility. When I chaired *The Brains Trust* one of
the questions, 'Do we have free will?', was hailed with glee by
the philosophers and theologians around the table. It evidently
comes up over and over in their very different professional
circles. The answer that emerged was that we can't be sure
which prevails in our making, certainly both nature and nurture play a huge part, but as moral beings it is imperative we
live our lives as though we do indeed have free will. That was
good enough for me.

Genes are among the many things I'm passing on. It's there
for all to see: fingernails, hair, toes, the timbre of voice . . .
all passed on from parents to children. Genetics had not
explained my damaged grandson; medicine was not advanced
enough for him. But he too shares our traits and something
of our temperaments. With so many other things in flux –
values, property, lifestyles, language – my genes seem to be
the surest of my legacies. Indeed they are my inheritance,
spinning on their way down the ages, living within others
who will not know nor care. As the year turns, I am content
with that.

On Patriotism

O n the shores of sleep I hear the church clock chime. It is a sweet sound, marking every hour throughout the night. The sound of it breaking through dreams and half-waking thoughts brings me comfort. Now it is eight in the morning and the low autumn sun is touching the scarlet Virginia creeper that clings to the wall across the lane. The chime is measured: each stroke occupying its full space, in no hurry to move on to the next. Each reverberation falls away across the tombstones just soon enough to give way to the next. There is no hurry, yet time will keep on passing. I lie in bed and let it pace my day.

———

War simplifies many things. For those running it, of course, it is very complex and challenging and exhilarating. Which is why so many veterans speak of it as the best years of their lives. For those simply enduring war, matters are simple: survival, resilience, care for those immediately close. Many of my values forged during the Second World War have endured because they were so fiercely important. None more so than patriotism. And being a child at the time, its power sank deep.

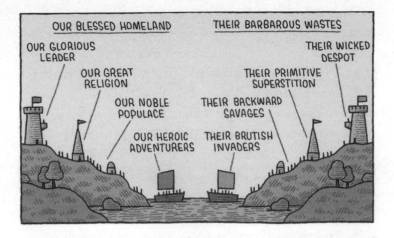

The first principle of patriotism seemed to be 'our side is better than the rest'. It is an easy emotion. Patriotism is like that: once you get it, you don't have any problems. You react predictably to the flag, the national anthem, the monarchy, soulful poems about the father/motherland. Later you come to feel a sense of community with strangers met abroad with whom you have nothing else in common but an unquestioning love of the home country.

But as a child I wasn't going abroad. I wasn't going any-where except to Blackpool and the Lake District, and when the war ended Bournemouth and finally London. Europe was conceived as full of Germans doing bad things and righteous French, Dutch and Russian people doing good things. There was also the royal family visiting bomb sites and Myra Hess giving concerts at the National Gallery. I was shielded from, or possibly too young to comprehend, such things as the black market, the accident in Bethnal Green Tube station, where 173 people died in a crush on the stairs, or doubts cast over the bombing of Dresden and the atom bombs on Japan. Keep it simple, the message seemed to be, and you're ours for life.

And so it has proved: that visceral attachment of seemingly unqualified loyalty still has its hold. But it has had to face many challenges. I still have a lurch of feeling at the sound of Elgar's *Pomp and Circumstance*; I get a lump in my throat at the lyric 'Who were born of thee', and I feel a surge of pride when I sight the white cliffs of Dover. My teenage passion for Rupert Brooke still lingers over that 'corner of a foreign field'.

I know that nostalgia is a powerful part of this, as it is with much that goes through the mind of someone in their eighties. Nostalgia for something I have lost, lost maybe without regret, but something that is simply missing in a part of my life where once there was something. A gap, a vacancy . . . a place to be filled that the noise of contemporary life doesn't satisfy. So nothing wrong with nostalgia as long as we recognise it as such, a hazy recollection rendered poignant by memory.

My patriotism suffered many blows as I came to know about Britain's part in the world. I swung from the euphoric enthusiasm of victory to a mood of despairing disappointment. In the post-war era, with many countries seeking and gaining their independence, there was a widespread feeling that the empire was something to be ashamed of, that Britain had conquered swathes of the world for reasons of trade and power and these motives were somehow reprehensible. There were terrible freedom struggles in Malaya, Kenya, Cyprus; the independence and partition of India were catastrophically mishandled, and the arrival of loyal and aspiring citizens from the Caribbean was greeted in the rooming houses of our cities with cruelty and discrimination. And in the streets, and shops too. The immigrant communities from South-East Asia continue to face such treatment. It is not easy to be proud of your country when overt hostility damages so many lives.

So my patriotism has become more nuanced as I have got older. What remains almost unchanged is my love of the place itself. There is something so balanced, so equable about the British landscape: when it is not grand and awesome it has an unflamboyant beauty that impacts slowly on those who move within it. I can easily sound like a tourist brochure when I extol what I like about Britain: cathedral cities, winding little villages, broad downlands, craggy mountains, spreading river estuaries. But I like too the things that aren't so obvious: the fading road signs at country crossroads; the weathered tea shops fringing remote beaches; the cairns on mountain tops that exist without explanation; the faded grandeur of our seaside resorts – Llandudno, Scarborough, Brighton, Hastings, Weston-super-Mare. Among the many things I love are piers. And I love them with a passion. I am pleased to be a patron of the National Piers Society.

Seaside piers came into fashion in the nineteenth century and are uniquely British in their abundance: at the most recent count we have around fifty-five. Ryde on the Isle of Wight is the oldest, built in 1813 as a terminal for the mainland ferry and still used for that purpose today. Many are listed, some get Heritage Lottery Fund money. Private owners battle with the soaring costs of maintenance and insurance. Local councils rally round; loyal supporters set up rescue operations and somehow find the funds. Should we care? We enthusiasts believe we should.

Mostly piers are places to have a jolly time, strolling out above the sea, feeling momentarily free of the constraints of

*The piers at Blackpool,
Southwold, Clevedon
and Weston-super-Mare
(from top)*

landlocked living. There's something tantalisingly in-between about them. You leave dry land, bracing yourself against the sea breezes and setting your face to the prospect of being at sea. You can see between the planks the waves lashing below; you lean over the side for all the world as though you're on a cruise. Along the way there are benches to take the weight off your feet. There may be candy floss, what-the-butler-saw machines, even a tea room. At the end there's usually a clutch of fishermen. A stroll along the pier is one better than a stroll along the prom and every bit as traditional as the Mediterranean *passeggiata*. The reward, a panoramic view of the coastline you are leaving behind.

Piers aren't all the same, of course. They have their character, their own proud style. As a child I knew Blackpool's three piers best: the North Pier always sedate, the South Pier proud of its naughty glamour. From Llandudno Pier you can see the fine curve of the Victorian seafront; from Teignmouth you have a great view of the town's harbour. Many piers began as stages for passing steamers, but that trade went away and left them to find new roles.

Often they were working-class entertainments, but these days they have diversified. Southwold is now the destination of choice for Suffolk's chic weekenders. Clevedon Pier – discreetly Grade I listed – was declared by John Betjeman the most beautiful pier in England. It stretches out into the Bristol Channel and its good binoculars help you sight passing ships. My family recently celebrated a birthday with a party in the restaurant at the end of the pier at Weston-super-Mare.

Always there is bad news. Piers seem plagued by sudden fires. Some were hit by wartime mines. Every year notice is given that another one may not survive. But survive they do. But for how long? I fear their old-fashioned delights don't fit the template of today's leisure industry, and if they did — with fast-food joints, clubs and music — then health and safety strictures could kick in and destroy the business plan. Valiant efforts are being made around the coasts to work out how to keep them going. But with what appear to be stronger winds and seas battling our shores, and annual talk of flooding, then the effort needed can only get greater.

I persist in believing they will survive. I recognise some stubborn British trait that wants these ancient pleasure domes loved for their antiquity, their often ramshackle grace, their persistent lack of purpose. Councils scour their books for funds to help them out; entrepreneurs weigh up the risks and find the odds tough. But these quirky places hoist between land and sea speak of English ways and English eccentricities: Gilbert and Sullivan meets *Oh! What a Lovely War!* Nothing more patriotic than that.

In the 1970s I went for the BBC's *Holiday* programme to report from the Balkans. I knew that Yugoslavia had been the scene of complex fighting in the Second World War: Croatia had been allied to the Axis powers of Italy and Germany and controlled by the Ustaše fascist movement. There had been large-scale massacres of Serbs, Jews, Muslims and Romani people. I knew too that the British adventurer/soldier Fitzroy Maclean (said to be one of the origins of James Bond) had been parachuted by Churchill behind the German lines to join up with the partisans led by Tito and spearhead Western support for the resistance campaign. After the war ended and Tito, the hero of the resistance, became president and managed to stay non-aligned during the Cold War, I was perhaps not alone in seeing Yugoslavia as an indomitable sovereign state and, I was soon to find, a place of great beauty.

We travelled, filming as we went, to Mostar, the ancient capital of Herzegovina, remarkable for its harmonious mix of East and West, Muslim and Christian. We focused our reporting on the old town, marvelling at the happy proximity of cultures. I recall the steady hum of small-scale hammering coming from the artisan shops shaping brass into innumerable objects for sale. I bought a many-ringed necklace there. We featured not only mosques and churches but, most conspicuously, the great Mostar bridge, ordered by Suleiman the Magnificent in 1566 when the Ottomans held sway and a legendary piece of Islamic architecture. It spans ninety feet across the Neretva, made of stone and stepped like the Rialto Bridge in Venice. Indeed it has a similar significance as an emblem of its city.

In 1992 I was back in Yugoslavia, except it wasn't Yugoslavia any more. After Tito's death in 1980 the six constituent republics that had made up the country began to assert their right to independence. The country was engulfed by a civil war in which Yugoslav fought Yugoslav in their struggle to become independently Slovenian, Croatian, Bosnian, Serbian, Macedonian and Kosovar. The struggle was ferocious, with ethnic cleansing and war rape accepted as methods of conquest and millions displaced from their homes. By 1992 Europe stood appalled at the worst bloodshed and suffering since 1945. NATO was called on to intervene.

On 20 May 1992 I was on a flight to Zagreb with a film crew and producer for *Heart of the Matter*. At the airport I was immediately confronted with my ignorance. I asked at a news stand in the concourse for a map of the country. What I was given showed a strangely shaped land, with a long coastline of many islands and then, not far behind the coastal lands, its eastern border curving north and only descending south again beyond what was of course the bulging presence of Serbia. I was half inclined to go back and ask for a map of the entire country . . . meaning Yugoslavia, not just Croatia. But this was the new reality, in maps and on the ground. Croatia had declared independence in 1991. It was itself an entire country, and we were here because it was under attack from Serbia.

We hired a large camera van, took on board a Croatian cameraman who'd been filming the war for months and knew his way around, and drove south towards the fighting in Vukovar. I have never seen rows of smouldering buildings before. They were modest roadside houses with gardens and children's toys, and small farms with fences and bedraggled crops. The people had gone. Some stretches of road had houses charred from earlier forays. This went on and on as we drove south. Neighbour had turned against neighbour, rallying to the extremist slogans of Slobodan Milošević calling for a revival of the greater Serbia as it had existed centuries before. At the same time Croatia's first president, Franjo Tuđman, voiced intentionally offensive hatred of the Serb minority. This was rampant nationalism, a pride in their own country turned to fanatical hatred of the other.

Laudable patriotism is a good thing. It gives a wholesome sense of who we are, a sense of roots in our culture, language and customs. I had seen that on my former visit when different groups lived side by side in Sarajevo. But something poisonous can happen during an era of sudden historic change. Resentments that have festered for centuries can be stirred by those with political ambitions into a powerful nationalism that believes in its own superiority. There seems to be a very fine line easily crossed when rhetoric and passion stretch loyalty.

We were to find refugees bewildered by what was happening in the many camps that had sprung up. Women, young girls and children had been accommodated, but the menfolk had been held back. I spoke with teenage girls who were deeply distressed: 'I was always Yugoslav, we were all Yugoslav. That's how I am. But what is happening now, it's dreadful.' Civil war cuts people off from proper news, so rumours flourish. And the more hideous the better. I was told in all seriousness that Serbs were putting babies in tumble driers and spinning them to death. Where hatred and fear prevail nothing is too terrible to believe . . . or perhaps even to do. Nazi atrocities prove as much. We returned with our report and eventually the wars came to an end. I learned later that the Mostar bridge had been blown up in 1993 as the Croatians laid a ten-month siege to the eastern part of the town, expelling all the Bosnians and destroying all the mosques. Our resourceful cameraman had been killed a few months after we left.

There has been much patriotism/nationalism since the 1990s. The Arab Spring sounded a brave and refreshing movement. We in the West thought the uprisings signified a people wanting to install democratic governments where once there had been tyranny. We have learned since that they really sought to replace the existing tyranny with their own power structures, gaining some legitimacy from elections but quickly collapsing into rivalries fuelled by tribal hatreds. Libya, Egypt, Syria, all have fallen to the delusion that patriotic loyalties will bring the changes people want. In the end too many people want different things.

Now my own country is in the thick of it. My own country. Which is that, exactly? I would once have said it was Britain. I would have said it with confidence. But if asked now by a stranger abroad showing mild interest I think I would say I was English. Nationalism has come home, and with the move by Scottish people to have an independent country I am confronted with a new prospect. I am having part of my identity challenged. What I had assumed was part of being British is now saying it wants not to be so. This leaves me with a sense of hollowness. I look around and see it must be so.

I know countries I once took for granted – Czechoslovakia, Yugoslavia – are no longer entities. Their long histories have come full circle and demanded change. Scotland is doing the same. Their history which I thought was mine, that I learned at school: the bloody dynastic wars, Bruce and Wallace against Edwards I and II; James I uniting the crowns after the death of Elizabeth; the Enlightenment, with men of genius setting new ways of thinking, their men of invention transforming industry and communications. It is Holyrood Palace, where Darnley had the Queen's musician Rizzio killed; the Highland clearances driving crofters off the land; the Stuart challenge; the brutality of Culloden. But it had always been my unquestioning assumption that we were one. It is how life went. My uncle served with the Argyll and Sutherland Highlanders during the Second World War; I have reported for the national broadcaster from sixteen Edinburgh Festivals. I have made programmes with outstanding artists and writers – Ian Hamilton Finlay, Hugh MacDiarmid – about its opera and dance companies, and the creation of the Scottish Parliament. And now many people in this lovely country feel separate from me in ways that matter.

I can see independence must be allowed to happen if people want it. But I am left bereft at the prospect, weakened as if I had had a severe loss of blood. Get over it! If it happens of course I shall. My loss is modest enough compared to those fleeing their countries from fear or need. As frontiers shift and reshape, as nationalism slides to the extremes, as populations trek across the planet seeking safety, I have a sense of the great frailty of man. Nationality has corralled us into different spaces on the landmass; we have fought over those spaces to call them our own. We have defended and challenged those who would take by violence what we believe to be ours. But nothing is for ever. As empires come and go, that which is within us feels first a love, then a hurt, finally a resilience and resignation in the face of what is happening. At my age you learn all things change. That is the first law.

―

The apples are heavy on the trees, loading down the branches towards the grass. There is abundance this year, each garden bearing swags of ripening fruit. Many have already fallen to the ground where greedy insects gorge on the juices. I used to fear autumn as the season of dying. Now I see it as the season of fecundity. Here are the fruits of the early sap and flowers, the golden hoard offered up as some kind of benison to the earth. The round of nature is perpetual. I consider my place in it. On the whole I am pleased to have come to my harvest years.

On Language

The seasons are changing too, their rhythm unstoppable. Autumn trees are in full leaf. They are weighed by their load, towards the river, towards the grasses. In puddles of gold the conkers split and glow around the trunks of the horse chestnuts, exposing the pale pulpy hollow of their shells. On every branch each leaf is making its own transition from one season to another. Some still hold the full green of summer, others touched with bronze around their edges begin to feel the pinch of decay; yet others blaze, the full flags of a transformation. Underfoot they heap and bunch, ready for the children to kick around with their coloured boots. I watch one float slowly down to the surface of the river and drift away. I turn to go indoors, thoughtful.

—

I settle in the gloaming to think about how language has changed in my lifetime . . . how we speak differently, load words with different meaning. I've lived long enough for part of that evolving to have gone on in my adult life. Using words and language to earn my living, from time to time I have had to make conscious adjustments to keep up. But this becomes harder as I get older: I can sometimes forget new uses and emphases. I forgot the other day that 'rainbow' is in common use as a reference to multiethnicity and gender plurality.

However, the movement isn't always in one direction. Sometimes the old themselves are subject to glib and careless assumptions.

I have long been troubled by a British road sign that is meant to be helpful. It shows two figures, a man and a woman, leaning on walking sticks and looking both helpless and miserable. It is meant to alert motorists to the possibility of decrepit old people crossing the road more slowly than they, the motorists, would like. I doubt whether it does any good at all. But it certainly perpetuates the image of the old as weak and helpless, which, although some of us are, and increasingly as we get older, is not how we primarily see ourselves. The two old crones crossing are simply unhelpful when there are more than a million people over sixty still in work, and sprightly geriatrics running in the London Marathon. The language of traffic hieroglyphs fails us.

Signs are a crude way of conveying simple messages. They are not always accurate. I am always bemused by the signs on the doors of public toilets in the UK – these must be among the most coy and idiotic symbols in public use. 'His' and 'hers' have been tricked out in sly and winsome ways of separating the sexes: Romeo/Juliet, a knight in armour/maiden in distress, king and queen. Sometimes they are witty: I like XX and XY. The one that is most universal and irritates me most depicts the man as an upright, plainly two-legged figure and the female in what is meant to indicate a skirt: a ballooning triangular shape that extends from the waist and reaches its baseline somewhere around the knees. This is not how women have ever dressed, and even if it were its symbolic representation, symbolic of what? The fact is that women more often wear trousers as they go about the world today. I had an argument about this with a male friend who took on my challenge: we sat on the concourse of Euston station counting the women in trousers or leggings as against the women in anything that could be called a dress. The trousers were in a majority of three to one – so can we have new signs on our toilets, please. The one I truly like cuts to the truth: representing Women with stylised breasts, and the Men with a stylised penis.

But now comes rescue from social media. A website called 'It Was Never a Dress' has reconfigured the woman to have an entirely new identity, that of a caped superwoman. Its design was created for Axosoft by Tania Katan and the campaign is bold and witty, and has my support.

And so we come to words and to grammar. It is clearly important that at any given moment words carry exactly the same meaning for all who use them. It would be impossible to draw up a contract or negotiate an international treaty if words meant even slightly different things to different people. It may well be that addenda and footnotes are needed to make absolutely clear what is being agreed. Otherwise definitions could well be the subject of legal wrangles, international disputes and commercial misunderstandings. And they are. So grammar matters.

On the other hand in broader use – in discourse, light journalism, fiction – the rules can and are waived or ignored in accordance with the mood of what is being said. So on the one hand the users of language know there are absolute and agreed rules of grammar that can be crucial to interpretation, and on the other that casual talk, slang and popular culture will use that same language exactly as they please . . . breaking rules either from carelessness, fun or indifference, and not giving a damn. In daily life we swim between both.

It is a subject that over the generations divides families, provokes editors and irritates many – of whom I am one. Notice that 'whom': a word falling out of use in the present day, when concision is all and few people were taught as I was that 'who' refers to the subject of the verb and 'whom' is used as the object of the verb and always after a preposition. Does it matter? It certainly drives the grammar purists mad. Other solecisms include split infinitives, ending sentences with a preposition, and the proliferation of apostrophes in places where they don't belong. I'm with the purists on all these issues, but also mindful that language changes, and must change to stay alive. Sometimes I'm irritated, sometimes indifferent. Never unaware.

Today language is under ever-quickening change for two reasons: first, the deluge of new words; and second, the short cuts, jokes and abbreviations popular on the internet. Developments in technology, science and medicine, as well as the more fanciful inventions of social media, make it clear that the language must expand. Each year the Oxford Dictionary admits newcomers to its online pages and every quarter publishes the latest updates. Here are some relatively recent additions: duck face, lolcat, frack, man crush, hawt, detox and, more recently still, cisgender, crowdfunding, staycation, totes. The latest include binge-watch and dadbod. It is easy to imagine the language running away with itself, proliferating so fast that whole areas of definition will be understood only by special groups. This is already the case within medicine, pharmacology, the deep internet.

As for Twitter, I struggle to keep up. New acronyms are being invented every day. I think, on reflection, older people should keep out of it. They can only make fools of themselves. Remember David Cameron's e-mail to Rebekah Brooks? He added, by way of familiarity, 'lol', thinking it stood for lots of love. The Twittersphere collapsed in mockery: didn't he know it stands for laugh out loud? But this is an old story; things have probably moved on by now. The trick with social media is always to be several moves ahead. It asserts immediate authority and mocks the stragglers. However, I do have my own favourites: some years ago John Rentoul, stalwart journalist with a caustic view of newspaper behaviour, launched the hashtag #QTWTAIN. It stands for Question to Which the Answer is No, and is used to lampoon popular papers' love of headlines such as WAS JFK KILLED BECAUSE OF HIS INTEREST IN ALIENS? So many QTWTAIN responses followed that he published a book of them. Such vigilance and mockery do our language good.

At the same time, words are falling out of use. I situate myself among those whose vocabulary is loaded with what was current years ago. Example: for the Sky Arts Portrait Artist of the Year television programme Frank Skinner and I travel the country meeting artists whose skills are good enough to put them in contest. We have three judges from the art world and they make the choices. On one occasion, as Frank and I left the scene of discussion I said, 'We'll leave you to your deliberations.' Frank turned to me, smiling: 'Who uses a word like "deliberations" any more?' Well, I do, and I was taken aback by his comment. 'Deliberations?' A bit pompous perhaps. Too many syllables? I could have said thoughts, but deliberations means more than that. Still, I could see that my vocabulary is very largely set by language as I have lived it. One can only imagine how silly it would sound if I started spouting rap-speak or using emojis in my e-mails. (Sorry, I realise the use of 'one' to refer to oneself is archaic too, reserved only for top royals: 'One is not amused.')

Recent years have seen an explosion in the use of emojis, those cheeky little figures that express a range of stereo-typed reactions – happiness, fear, success, celebration. The notion came from the Japanese decades ago, but has spread since Apple started featuring them on their equipment. They pop up as an option on my tablet when I'm writing in good old-fashioned letters. There's clearly a new, quick and – to my mind – simplistic language emerging for the young and those in a hurry. In fact, we're back to the hieroglyphics we began with.

———

Some words are surviving vividly today, but with meaning totally different from the ones they had formerly. 'Gay' is the most obvious. When I first became aware of homosexuality, which was when I was at Cambridge in the 1950s, homosexuals were referred to as 'queers' and the more extravagant ones as queens. I was startled but not shocked by the attitude of the university community to what was still against the law. My boyfriend at the time, later my husband, was a student at King's College, and I studied economic history there with my supervisor, the historian Eric Hobsbawm, who had rooms in the Gibbs Building. Both were resolutely heterosexual. But I came to know many of their friends and associates who were not. E. M. Forster himself was still living in the Wilkins Building, and presumably nursing his unpublished novel *Maurice* – unpublished because it dealt with love between men. Among the senior figures at King's, the Provost Sir John Sheppard, Dadie Rylands, a fellow and scholar in the English Faculty and presiding spirit of the Marlowe Society, and the unassuming but delightful music scholar Philip Radcliffe were all 'out' (as we say now). In my own student generation the brilliant gadfly Julian Jebb was flamboyantly gay; he borrowed my dresses to go to parties. But 'out' and 'gay' were no part of their vocabulary.

'Cool' once meant not warm: it still does. But younger people use it – overuse it – as a word of approval for anything considered enviably fashionable or sophisticated. 'Goth' once referred to the invading tribes of Eastern Europe who reached and sacked Rome in AD 410. And even in that one phrase I have betrayed my age: who talks about the sacking of a city any more? Certainly not the contemporary reporters speaking of attacks on Tikrit or Kobanê. And it is no longer considered correct to refer to the years numbered from the Christian era as AD – Anno Domini, in the year of the Lord. This tradition is of medieval European origin and is meant to measure years from the conception of Christ. There is no year zero: 1 BC is followed immediately by AD 1. But the tradition is fading. BC/AD measures time according to one specific religion at the expense of others. In the spirit of tolerance such time is now increasingly referred to as CE, the Common Era, and BCE, Before the Common Era.

'Goth', meanwhile, has developed a vivid contemporary meaning. Goth rock describes a type of music that came along in the late 1970s, after punk, and seemed harsher, darker, noisier. The prototype I knew was the band Siouxsie and the Banshees: their singer a strident, confident young woman who made a great impact on my teenage daughter. A good role model, I thought. Goth followers became, like their European antecedents, an identifiable tribe: young people clad in dark clothes, purples and blacks, darker make-up, black nails, lavish body piercings, and in some an inclination to cut themselves.

'Coloured' presents a different shift of meaning, and one that takes us into delicate political territory. There is no word that currently so defines the gap between the generations, the older ones being familiar with earlier usage, the younger finding that usage positively offensive. In the 1960s the American civil rights movement was powerful in commanding our loyalties and support. But I lived at a distance from their felt political involvement. I had grown up speaking of negroes and had to learn that it caused offence. There was even a colour, 'nigger brown': Stevie Smith uses it in her *Novel on Yellow Paper* published in 1936. As a young adult in the 1950s I knew this, by then, was totally unacceptable. All along we have had to unlearn, and learn the new usage from those who saw it as the language and vocabulary of their oppressors. I have been happy to do so, but as the years go by I find I'm slower than I was at catching up. Hence the problem has to be spelled out for me. Nowhere have I seen it done better than by fellow Labour peer Oona King, who responded vigorously when some time ago the actor Benedict Cumberbatch, speaking up for actors who he felt deserved better career opportunities, referred to them as 'coloured'. There were cries of outrage to which Oona replied:

Benedict Cumberbatch deserves thanks for dipping his toe into the troubled waters of broadcasting diversity. He raised the thorny issue of his black acting friends not getting the same opportunities as white actors, particularly here in the UK. His accidental use of the derogatory term 'coloured' promptly flung him into the linguistic swamp that mires race. This swamp is conscientiously patrolled by the PC diversity brigade, and as a reward Benedict's had his head bitten off – a sort of linguistic version of sharia.

As a diversity executive with Channel 4 (often viewed as a member of the PC brigade) I realise I too will have my head bitten off for writing that last sentence. And as someone who studied Islam at university, and has a great respect for that religion, I know there are too many lazy and ignorant interpretations of sharia in the press. But here's the point: too often we get overly exercised by individual words, or throwaway lines, instead of stepping back to see the wider meaning.

Don't get me wrong. I understand the importance of language. As a mixed-race person who grew up labelled 'half-caste', I knew those words stained and demeaned me. But when my white gran, for example, used the term 'half-caste', it wasn't because she thought I was inferior or wanted me to leave the country. She left school at 13, worked in a cigarette factory, never met a black man until my Mum married one, and only ever heard mixed-race people referred to as half-caste. It was all she knew.

I recognise that Benedict − educated at Harrow, and whose great-grandfather was a consul general for Queen Victoria − has less ignorance to fall back on. But he works in America where most black people refer to themselves as 'people of colour', and he no doubt conflated that with 'coloured people'. And he also may not realise why black people reject the term 'coloured': it is too closely associated with the evils of segregation and Jim Crow laws that enslaved an entire racial group.

For my black grandfather − born in 1893 in the Southern Bible Belt to parents who were little more than slaves − the term 'coloured' represented everything that dehumanised him.

I am grateful to Oona King for that. But for many of my age it still has to be spelled out: the correct word is 'black'.

Other words have lived on the cusp of change. How we refer to the disabled was and may remain problematic. In more cruel times such people could be called spastic, loony.

Not any more. It is one of the most wonderful improvements of our day that real effort is made to find the terms that do not insult people whose lives are impaired in some way. Sometimes in trying to define what's acceptable the language veers in the wrong direction and has to be brought back within the bounds of what is reasonable. It happened when the unmarried began openly living together: there was some awkwardness as to how to refer to them when introductions were being made. The term 'significant other' was tried out. It flopped. Now it comes perfectly easily to speak of a 'partner': how could it ever have been a problem? Likewise the term disabled is now universally acceptable: it features on all the Blue Badge literature. There was a moment when 'less abled' was given an airing. That too simply faded away.

There are words, then there's pronunciation. They are each changing all the time, of course, but never before have changes been so keenly monitored. Recordings, radio and television chart the changes throughout the twentieth century. I grew up knowing there was something called variously spoken English, the King's English, received pronunciation . . . and that it was not only desirable in itself, for reasons of class snobbery, but also important for career prospects and interviews. My mother was alarmed enough by my Stockport accent to send me for elocution lessons. I scored badly in every test.

At Cambridge I found myself surrounded by the honking

voices of public-school-educated girls who were amused by my northern tones. I was eager, not so much to cosy up to them, as to pass unnoticed, unremarkable. I felt the pressure so keenly that there came a moment when I decided to change. I hadn't time to do things gradually. I needed to get on with it. I remember going into the toilets (not lavatories, not loos), leaving my Stockport vowels behind and coming out speaking with the tight throat and pursed lips of the most ludicrous stage-posh. It was an act of gross impersonation. Or that's how it felt inside. Strangely, no one noticed, or if they did no one remarked on it. Until, that is, I went home to the suburban semi. My parents made no comment, but they were clearly bewildered: their exchanged glances indicated as much. It was obvious that my ludicrous posturing had no place in the home where I grew up.

Elocution wasn't meant to turn out like this. In the decades that followed, writers from working-class backgrounds would write novels and plays about how their university education had shunted them unwittingly into the middle classes and opened up a gulf separating them from the deep cultural roots of their parents. Richard Hoggart's 1957 classic *The Uses of Literacy* references these changes. He charted the move to mass culture as expressed in film, tabloids and advertising. He regretted the loss of the old local communities: he himself never lost his rich Yorkshire burr. His book signalled the beginning of a change that's been proceeding ever since towards a wider acceptance of different speech patterns and accents.

During the Second World War the BBC employed Wilfred Pickles as an occasional newsreader, in the belief his rich

Yorkshire accent would deceive listening Germans. But once the war was over BBC English prevailed again. In my own days as a studio manager at Broadcasting House I was put through the drill of an audition to see whether my voice was right for broadcasting wavelength announcements to countries behind the Iron Curtain. It wasn't. They never explained why, but I suspected the old Stockport lilt had crept back into my speech.

It was the rise of pop music that changed all that. From the 1960s, with the Beatles leading the way, the use of natural voice and speech became acceptable. Musicians from across the north – Lindisfarne, Alan Price and the Animals – each brought their own idiosyncratic style to their lyrics, their speech and their inflections. The public loved it. It was even rumoured that posh boys wanting to get in with the in-crowd would switch accents to be more popular. In the same decade a generation of actors, Albert Finney and Tom Courtenay among them, came from northern homes, bringing their voices with them, and made it in the new wave of films about working-class lads and lasses. The broadcasting world gradually let all sorts of voices take roles as DJs and presenters, though the ranks of managers remained stuffily correct. For my part, under competing pressures to both be myself and to get on in the world of broadcasting, I seem to have evolved a mid-range, nowhere-very-much voice that suited the times. It was a source of amusement when in the 2010s it was reported to me that, having been suggested to present a BBC radio programme, I was rejected because 'she sounds too posh'. My mother would have been proud.

—

These random thoughts comfort me by my autumn fireside. I gather kindling and newspaper and stack the logs on top. Outside there is a wind blowing and the first leaves are beginning to rattle around the garden. The sky is full of blown clouds and the treetops are swaying together: soon their leaves will be falling in golden masses and the paths will be full of their fall. I feel my own autumn coming on and resolve to savour its pleasures.

———

There remain in my life the mannerisms of language I simply cannot unlearn. For some reason parents plus teachers plus the early-twentieth-century grammar bible *Fowler's Modern English Usage* have left their mark. My copy of Fowler is reprinted, 'with corrections', in 1950. It's good to know that the tyrant of grammar could himself make mistakes. Here's an example of his grammatical tyranny and what we were battling with. It concerns the use of 'as if' and 'as though' in a conditional clause:

'These should', he declares, 'invariably be followed by a past conditional, and not by a present form. The full form of the incorrect *"It is scanned curiously as if mere scanning* will *resolve its nature"* is *"It is scanned curiously as it would be scanned if mere scanning* would *resolve its nature"* and the omission of *"it would be scanned"* leaves *would resolve* unchanged.'

This kind of precious hair-splitting has long gone out of fashion. What remains is my resistance to the now regular substitution of 'like' for 'as if' or 'as though' . . . 'It looks as if it will rain today'; 'it looks as though it might rain today' both pass my grammar test. 'It looks like it might rain today' seems to me totally wrong. I cannot use it myself and I wince whenever journalists and broadcasters use it, which they do, often. It must by now be received usage. But not with me.

And then there's the sat/sitting conflict. I was always taught in my grammar lessons that any continuous past action required the present participle; thus 'I was sitting at the window' is correct. 'I was sat at the window' was quite wrong. Popular usage has now made 'I was sat' acceptable. The only people it irritates – apart from grammar fanatics – is people like me who made all the effort years ago to learn the rules. I find myself correcting a grandchild . . . it's 'sitting' not 'sat' . . . only to be faced with amazed disbelief. What can it possibly matter, as long as the meaning is clear? I realise there is no chance of retrieving the old rules simply because grammar isn't taught like that any more. I doubt if the grandchild knows what 'continuous past' and 'present participle' are. Why should they? Teachers, rules, usage have all changed, and with it the language. It's I as elder citizen who is struggling to keep up. Or perhaps that could be 'it's me'?

On Bodies

The insects are coming in for the winter. The other evening I went out for a final look at the night sky and as I opened the latched door a sturdy little spider came rattling over the tiles, for all the world as if it had been standing impatiently waiting for me to answer its summons. It moved at a terrific pace, scuttling purposefully towards a rug. I watched its progress in amazement at such energy and intent from so tiny a creature. Another evening I returned to find a hornet buzzing angrily up in the room's elm beams. My switching on the light drove it into a frenzy. It clearly didn't want to be there and nor did I want it. We engaged forces; it with increased noise and agitation and I with a rolled newspaper. Slowly I manoeuvred it towards the door and eventually out into the night.

The autumn evenings are closing in. The air is still balmy but the sense of decline haunts the hedges and trees. I sit by the river watching the drift of leaves down towards the green sluggish water. The time to come indoors arrives earlier and earlier for me as well as for the insects.

—

Last summer I fell out of the window. Not deliberately. I was simply being careless. It happened to be the tall sash window that opens directly onto the tiny balcony of my London home so there was no tragic fall and splat on the pavement.

There was, however, a splat on the sill. I was carrying a tray of drinks and came crashing across the sash window. Not having a hand free to steady myself I simply sprawled full length: glasses – the drinking kind – went flying. Glasses – seeing kind – fell onto the tray. But nastily my shins were raked by the wood of the window frame, the skin torn and the flesh gouged. I winced with the pain.

Living on my own, I had to manage my own accident. I pulled myself back into the room and dumped myself for ten minutes or so on the sofa. I needed to collect myself and assess the damage. I was shaken, that was clear. The fine day quivered outside but I was shivering with shock. I waited to see if anything happened; it did. My legs stretched out before me began to swell: the line of my shinbone grew into marked and ungainly lumps. They were painful to the touch and felt puffy and unreal. I was able to get to my feet, no bones broken, and I fetched ice lumps from the freezer, wrapped them in two tea towels and lay on the sofa with one clasped to each shinbone. The ice took away the pain. But it began to melt and I began to get bored. I fetched a book and read it for about an hour. By then the lumps had subsided a good deal and I was able to clear things up . . . tray, shards of glass, myself.

In the days that followed scabs grew along my shins. I administered arnica regularly. The scabs peeled away leaving pale vulnerable skin. Weeks passed; the pale skin darkened. Months passed and the scar is still there. The ageing body doesn't restore itself with the swift exuberance of youth. Perhaps these scars are with me for ever. Will some archaeologist disinter my bones and, finding scratches on ancient shinbones, speculate about a cycling accident, a mountain fall, domestic brutality? I became charmed by the idea that my marked bones will take their story . . . the wrong story . . . into the future.

Your best chance of your body's recognisable traces surviving comes if you fall into a bog, more especially a peat bog. It's been discovered that its chemical constituents are such that not only is the skeleton preserved but so often are the fleshy parts and the organs, hair, fingernails and scraps of clothing. A whole group of such survivors known to archaeologists as the bog people has offered up fascinating details of their lives that no set of bones alone could yield. Their research is rich ground, literally, for finding out about diet, health and, often gruesomely, how they died. But there is another aspect of what are today museum showstoppers: they allow ordinary mortals, not preoccupied with bog acids and pH levels, to look directly into the faces, the individual features, of those who lived centuries, even millennia, before they did.

Tollund Man is one of the most renowned, most studied and most complete of such bog people. He was discovered in Denmark in 1950 and dated at around 400 BC. His is a long square face, with a fine textured skin not yet wrinkled around the mouth or nose. He has a large narrow nose, its nostrils finely shaped; his eyes sit close upon his nose – rather as Prince Charles's do – and they are closed as in sleep. His mouth is wide but narrow-lipped, the lower lip more full than the upper. He would have a broad smile. Did Neolithic and Iron Age man smile? We never think of his doing so. No recreated models or pictorial versions show him or them enjoying a joke. Had humour been invented then, did our ancestors roam the wild scrubland shouting jokes about the dinosaur that crossed the road, and crazy explanations of how the mammoth got its tusks? Tollund Man doesn't look the type who would have done so, because close above his nose and cutting into his otherwise smoothly skinned forehead are two deep-set furrows. Did he worry them there? And what constituted worry in an Iron Age life? Or was the furrowed brow an instant and puzzled reaction to the sudden and cruel death about to befall him?

Because this is not simply a skull, but a fully fleshed head and face. Its expression reaches out his humanity to touch us. It reminds me of the expression of those I have loved and cradled in their last hours, an expression yielding to the habit of pain and an acceptance – half regretful, half resigned – of their impending death.

This is mere imagining on my part because the findings about the bog people allow of no such fancy. Enough of them have now been unearthed – some hundreds, mostly in Northern Europe, especially Denmark, Germany and Ireland – for certain generalisations to be made. A large number are judged to be between the ages of sixteen and twenty: they appear not to have been unwell at the time of death and were often well-nourished and even, in the case of Lindow Man, well-manicured. It has been widely speculated – verification must be elusive – that these were human sacrifices made to the gods. Either that, or the execution of those guilty of deviant behaviour. It is possible that for some peoples the bog itself, with its strange consistency, half earth, half water, might be seen as some transitional space to the next world. Many bodies bear the marks of violent blows; Tollund Man came to the light of later day with the rope of his strangulation still around his neck.

I enter by the back door, knowing the great front entrance will be clogged with tourists, students, visitors. Later I see them, queue-long waiting to have their bags checked. I get through at a skip and then wend my way through all the sumptuous rooms to the Great Court, Norman Foster's triumphant space now housing a grand circling shopping area, several counters and cafés for food, and, looking almost apologetically out of place, the wonderful Roman equestrian statue of a young man. I make for the enquiries desk where they provide at once all the details of what I seek. Yes, on the third floor, Room 50, the lift's over there, turn left when you come out and the rooms are straight ahead. The British Museum at its best. I share the lift with two Asian girls. We have skirted two school crocodiles – the tidier one in the crisp navy and white blazers of a private school; the second less dragooned in brightly coloured tabards proclaiming the name of their state primary. Up on the third floor things are quieter, the school parties here more subdued, overwhelmed perhaps by the scale and sheer authority of the displays. And a good many of them are paying close attention to Roman and Celtic artefacts.

But no one is bothering with Lindow Man. I have him to

myself. Here he is, fetched up among the murmuring excitement of Western museum life, a small but significant trophy
in the world's greatest collection. I am startled that he is so
small: a crumpled shred of a man lying in the agonies of his
death. He has been placed on a layer of what might, appropriately, be peat. The low ceiling to his heat-controlled display
cabinet has discreet lighting, as though fearful of disturbing
him. Stronger light had earlier been shown to bleach his skin.
His bones have found a quiet corner.

But the flesh of his face writhes in the instant of pain as it hit
him. He is caught in the moment. His blond hair is clamped to
his skull, which bears a small hole. The flesh that folds round
his neck is leathery and brown. It is the peat that has preserved
him. The scourge of time that strips the flesh and leaves only
bone has no play here. Here is flesh: bog flesh.

I grew up in that part of Cheshire which borders
Lancashire. Not far away from my home was the thriving
village of Wilmslow, in the 1940s already a rather upmarket
suburban settlement with detached houses and good shops. I
didn't know it had a bog, or even that there was a place in the
fields around called Lindow Moss. There was no reason why
I should because it was by all accounts a bleak and deserted
place. As the glaciers of the Ice Age melted they dumped sand,
gravel and clay on the Cheshire Plain. It evolved into a huge
peat bog that once covered some fifteen hundred acres. In
1421 the lords of the manor allowed local people to dig peat
for fuel and it seems they have been digging ever since. Only
the landless poor, gypsies and Irish peat-cutters ever made
their homes there. By 1970 all trace of dwellings had gone.
But peat-cutting was thriving business.

On 1 August 1984 peat-cutters found bones: a human leg. Police were notified and the county archaeologist was on site the next day. Lindow Man was about to see the light. Five days later the slab of peat containing his remains was lifted and taken to the mortuary at Macclesfield District General Hospital. The local coroner and police checked it out, but by 17 August carbon dating had determined the peat was at least a thousand years old. So no murder inquiry was called for. Meanwhile the landowners had given the remains to the British Museum, whose expert team went to work. He acquired the nickname Pete Marsh, but was formally put on show as Lindow Man. He has proved a steady attraction ever since. I hover round the display, leaning across to confront the face as closely as possible. He is a young man in his mid-twenties who met a violent death, possibly in a ritual killing as was the case for other bog men across Europe. It has no significance for me, of course, but I am intrigued by how

Tollund Man

just occasionally a body, a skull, a face, an individual survives the centuries. And here he is emerging into our own time, his screaming face struggling to tell his tale.

He's not the only one. Other bodies or parts of bodies have been found on Lindow Moss: the first discovery was made in 1983, when the skull of a young woman came to light. The police were investigating an unsolved murder at the time and interviewed a suspect whose home had bordered the Moss. The suspect at first denied all knowledge, until the police revealed the discovery of the skull whereupon he confessed. His timing was unfortunate for carbon dating subsequently revealed it was around eighteen hundred years old. They have clearly been killing people for centuries in that part of Cheshire.

———

Today nature is as still as I have known it. So I walk down the green lane round the yew tree to sit on the bench over-looking the river. I have neither sauntered nor rushed. I am in no hurry. I have all the time in the world. But yet I haven't. None of us has all the time in the world. We each have a brief snatch of air and space and then are gone. So why hurry?

The water is green, flowing slowly under leaning trees not yet promising the leaf to come. The water is still but chang-ing; edging round a clump on the opposite bank it divides and spreads in a consistent pattern: the water flows on, the pattern remains. It settles the mind. I return to my desk.

———

I go in search of my own skull. It must be here somewhere. When you look in a mirror it's hard to see.

Groomed for decades by multi-million-pound cosmetics advertising, we know to spot the first signs of a sagging chin, bags under the eyes, wrinkles at the corners (too much laughing!). Fashions in facial styles will betray our age: if we were of the generation that went in for the lean, sharp look of plucked eyebrows we may find we are stuck with them when the style evolves . . . a living-out of our mother's warning against an ugly face: 'You'll get stuck with it if the wind changes!'

Throughout my lifetime the ways of adorning and elaborating the human face and the human body have multiplied. Many have brought old traditions back into favour. The plucking of eyebrows goes back to the Egyptians and eyebrow threading comes from old Indian ways. Tattooing, once the preserve of hearty merchant sailors, now produces its own hierarchy of tattoo artists and the body art movement with its own stars and masterpieces. I know of a British painter who has Leonardo da Vinci's drawing of the bones of the foot tattooed across her own. Piercing has spread from eyebrows to cheeks, to lips and tongues. Fingernails are now not simply adorned with a single colour but are the site of elaborate patterns involving glitter and other stuff. Tribal practices have made their way into the beauty parlours of the West. Burmese women once fixed numbers of coloured bands closely around their necks. Now they pose for tourist photographs. Earlobe extensions come with a warning they won't quickly revert to normal.

There now seems nothing that can shock. Yet the search goes on: the urge to stand out, to outrage, to startle, to claim commonality with a like-minded clique . . . these impulses have almost run out of options. But this is all surface stuff, exhausting the expanses of skin wherever it reaches, elaborating life rather than confronting death. Few of us consider the skull.

But some do. The skull is darker stuff. It will survive us when hair and skin have withered away. I look in the mirror to confront my own survival. I can't see it there; I grin and confront my teeth but still I can't conjure the skull beneath. I thrust my fingers through my hair, sensing and configuring the lumps, the raw stuff of Victorian phrenology. This pseudo-science was all the rage in the nineteenth century: Queen Victoria and Prince Albert had their children's heads read. So does the slight swelling above my left ear signify my finer judgement, and what about that awkward little bump at the nape of my neck? Then I remember school chums long ago cruelly snatching a stool away just as I was about to sit on it and the blood trickling down my neck as I sportingly pretended it was all good fun. A bump of mistrust then. And nothing to do with the bogus science.

It is the poets and artists who take the skull as the ultimate irreducible emblem of death. Written in his late twenties, the title of T. S. Eliot's poem 'Whispers of Immortality' glosses Wordsworth's own 'Intimations of Immortality'. Wordsworth's Ode is lyrical and romantic; Eliot's intimation is visceral, direct and brutal, dealing as a young man should simply with whispers rather than Wordsworth's more portentous intimations. What surprises me is that both refer to immortality, when what really spooks them is the idea of mortality. Here's Eliot:

Webster was much possessed by death
And saw the skull beneath the skin;
And breastless creatures under ground
Leaned backward with a lipless grin.

Daffodil bulbs instead of balls
Stared from the sockets of the eyes!
He knew that thought clings round dead limbs
Tightening its lusts and luxuries.

Donne, I suppose, was such another
Who found no substitute for sense,
To seize and clutch and penetrate;
Expert beyond experience,

He knew the anguish of the marrow
The ague of the skeleton;
No contact possible to flesh
Allayed the fever of the bone.

He cites Webster; he cites Donne. Webster, whose imagination was obsessively preoccupied with the horrors of human decay and death, of whom theatre critic Kenneth Tynan said, 'His muse drew nourishment from Bedlam, and might, a few centuries later, have done the same from Belsen.' And Donne, the great metaphysical poet who is said to have posed in his shroud for the design of the statue that stands in St Paul's Cathedral where he was dean. I am drawn to these grim responses to death. Not because I share them; I am not sure what my own response is. But because I find them totally authentic . . . a clear admission that death terrifies and offers no comfort.

In our own day the arch-exponent of that view is Damien Hirst. One of his most famous works, the thirteen-foot shark suspended in a tank of formaldehyde, is called *The Physical Impossibility of Death in the Mind of Someone Living*. The phrase sums up the spirit of all he does. We simply cannot get our heads round the matter. Philip Larkin's poem 'Aubade' set it out for his generation:

> I work all day, and get half-drunk at night.
> Waking at four to soundless dark, I stare.
> In time the curtain edges will grow light.
> Till then I see what's really always there:
> Unresting death, a whole day nearer now,
> Making all thought impossible but how
> And where and when I shall myself die.
> Arid interrogation: yet the dread
> Of dying, and being dead,
> Flashes afresh to hold and horrify.

I cannot talk with Webster or Donne or Eliot or Larkin. So I go to see Damien. I want to talk about the diamond skull, a platinum cast of a human skull encrusted with almost nine thousand diamonds, and declared by him to be worth £50 million. The price is intrinsic to his snook-cocking at the art market and his defiant place both within and beyond it. Worldly success has gone hand with hand with critical acclaim. His enterprise is global and his entrepreneurial skills both challenge and embrace the mendacity of today's grotesque prices. In 2008, sidelining his famous agents Larry Gagosian and Jay Jopling, he went directly to Sotheby's with an auction of his work that took £111 million. His central London powerhouse is a spacious place of light and air, splashed with bright and colourful art and manned by a staff of crisp and elegant women. We settle in lavish sofas. And the tale unfolds. Damien Hirst does not press his views upon you . . . he leaves his art to do that. So in teasing out his attitudes I feel I am crassly revisiting what is already known. But somewhere in our conversation the essence is crystallised: life and death is all there is.

'Death is the only black and white: everything else is grey.' He has known this since the age of seven, growing up to confront what can't be avoided. 'It's a good way of dealing with

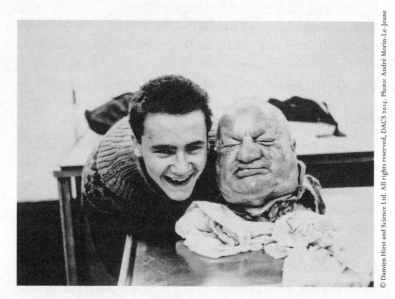

Damien Hirst, With Dead Head, 1991

it.' He certainly confronted it when as a sixteen-year-old he embarked on an art foundation course at Jacob Kramer College in Leeds: he would visit the university Anatomy Museum to practise drawing. Many students presumably did the same but few took it further. Damien had his photograph taken with his own head aligned beside that of a middle-aged man on the mortuary table. Damien's face is fresh, his expression cheeky; beside it, the severed head of the corpse is slumped, its flesh collapsed in folds. It must surely have felt cold to the touch. It is ghoulish, unsentimental, brazen. Hirst had the photograph framed and, called *With Dead Head*, it was first exhibited in 1991. Webster would surely have approved.

He had given up being a Catholic at the age of twelve, but the influence lingers. His work consistently makes use of Christian words and images. The diamond skull is called *For the Love of God*, a neatly ambiguous phrase hinting at possible recollections of his mother's impatience. A second skull — that of an infant, adorned with pink and white diamonds – is called *For Heaven's Sake*, another expression of exasperation but also invoking religious language. He had seen at the British Museum an Aztec skull encrusted with turquoise stones; he loves the Mexican approach to death, a sort of in-your-face directness that seeks to override sensations of pity and grief. 'Death is normal and it's a good way of dealing with it.' Hirst claims not to invent – 'I don't invent . . . I notice things' – but he also transforms.

The diamond skull is a cast of the skull of a young adult male, aged eighteen to twenty-four, probably dating – though this is challenged – from between 1720 and 1810. I ask how he came by the skulls. It seems you can buy these things at shops with names like Get Stuffed, a taxidermy business in Islington, and The Bone Room based in Berkeley, California, an internet natural history store that will sell you anything from a full human skeleton to an insect trapped in amber and the penis bone of a beaver.

Hirst chose a skull that appeared as typically a skull as possible; I take that to mean with no evident ethnicity. Research indicates it is of European/Mediterranean origin. He detached and cleaned the teeth and set them in the platinum jaw: their condition indicated the young man had experienced some health trauma between the ages of five and eight, possibly rickets or measles, or a more general and extended period of deprivation. Then he and his team of technicians encrusted the entire cast with 8601 flawless diamonds, filling even the eye sockets and nostrils. On the forehead is fixed a fifty-two-carat pear-shaped stone surrounded by fourteen smaller diamonds. In one of the design drawings, Hirst has scribbled: I once was / what you are / You will be / what I am.

Before I leave, Damien hands me a sheaf of photographs. They are work in progress, towards his next exhibition. I recognise the pictures: they are of the bog men . . . preserved and withered bodies of men ritually sacrificed. I am on familiar ground.

I feel I must decide whether to leave my body to science or not. Working as I have done for more than ten years on programmes about medical ethics, I have always been conscious that the traumas and crises we report could one day apply to me. Perhaps I should have been more detached, more objective. But the times of the stiff upper lip are past. We are constantly invited to feel and share. We live in times of personal involvement with each other: readers of newspapers identify with the distress of celebrities; readers of misery memoirs somehow find their own misery ameliorated; the death of Princess Diana had thousands sobbing for their own griefs. There's good and bad in this. First, there exists no contact: the idea of the shared trauma is bogus, an imaginative fiction. Yet we depend on empathy to keep going, to stand any chance of knowing how the world, and we in it, work. That is how I come to be tuned to the need for transplants, blood transfusions and all the ways the dead have of helping to heal the living.

There are degrees of disposing of one's body. You can leave instructions that your organs are to be made available for transplant. And you can go further: you can leave your body to medical science. The two options have ambushed my good intentions. I need to run them to ground.

Somewhere in the reaches of my memory is my joyous reaction on first seeing Stanley Spencer's painting *The Resurrection, Cookham*. How can you not smile? This huge painting is one of the favourites at London's Tate Britain. Here on this vast canvas – some eight feet by seventeen – is portrayed the moment when people rise from the dead: they are Stanley Spencer himself, his new wife and their neighbours and friends in Cookham churchyard. They are rising from the dead into the paradise that is the Cookham they have known and loved all their lives. The painting has delicious detail: everyone wears their ordinary day clothes, black velvet, a lace collar, a wife brushes down the soil from her husband's coat, a young girl smells a large sunflower, a crowd is taking a pleasure boat up the Thames. All is well, Spencer seems to be saying, in this world and the next.

Even as a small child with my innocent imagination and my Sunday-school knowledge I didn't think the resurrection would be like this. But I did wonder then, as many religious sects have since, whether at the last trump all the tombs would yield up their dead and we would need our limbs to see us on into eternity. You can see where this is heading.

No, I do not believe in the resurrection of the body, Christ's or anyone else's. I know it is the central belief of the Christian church, which churchgoers acknowledge devoutly and regularly when they recite the creed. I know too that for many it is this central tenet that makes Christianity a matter of faith and not of historic or metaphoric interpretation. I understand the story of doubting Thomas interpreted as 'proof' that Christ's resurrected body was genuinely flesh and blood and not any kind of vision seen by needy disciples. I know too that many

Stanley Spencer, The Resurrection, Cookham

sects of different faiths believe that what remains of you after your death needs to be treated with honour, preserved in particular rituals and stored with specific rites. I know too that many die unmarked, unloved and unmourned. All this I know.

I know, too, there is no explanation for death and that in the immediate world there is suffering: I have seen the grief of those close to someone who is dying. There is no answer.

In the 1980s the Scottish artist John Bellany was growing frail; his earlier years of heavy drinking were behind him but their effects were not. His paintings, once a joyous riot of colour, had transmuted into an array of pastel and pale shades. They, like him, were losing their vigour. He needed a liver transplant. When the operation was over and his recovery, dependent on a vast array of tablets, was in full swing we talked of the person whose liver he had inherited. John was almost viscerally aware of the presence within his body of another identity: 'I think he must have liked classical music: I have never been drawn to Tchaikovsky before, or to Stravinsky.' John loved the piano and no day went by without him sitting to play, but now he was playing a new and different repertoire. He saw this as the gift of his donor: with the life-saving liver had come a shift in musical taste, one that John welcomed, even relished as in the nature of their shared organ.

John was a great romantic, a man of passions and wild expression. After the transplant his paintings once more exploded with colour and energy . . . again a development he credited to his unknown benefactor.

There is, as far as I know, no medical evidence that taste

or preferences can travel from one individual to another parcelled in a transplant. However, in the world of the imagination who is to say what exchanges might pass as the flesh of one is subsumed into the flesh of another. It is part of medical etiquette that the names of patient and donor or their families are not exchanged. But I can't help feeling that those who were grieving their loss might take a muted comfort from knowing what the person whose life they saved made of it all.

I have made a living will. Nowadays it is called an advance directive – was there ever such a triumph of bland bureaucracy-speak as this? I persist in calling it a living will. In it I set out what my wishes are should I by an accident or illness no longer be able to convey my medical preferences. I recommend everyone over sixty do the same. We never know when we might be forestalled by a speeding lorry or a clogged artery.

Medical science is able to work wonders, and one of those wonders might be its capacity to keep you alive longer than you would want. Younger people – and many up-to-date doctors are young – seem to believe in life at any price. As the years go by and the length of life ahead begins to look shorter that view often mellows. I was shocked, in my forties, visiting an ailing aunt to have her whisper to me, 'I'm ready to go, Joan. I'm quite ready.' Now I'm in my eighties I understand. Those thrusting young medics, so brilliant in their skills, so up-to-the-minute with their diagnoses and drugs, so adept at their resuscitation and intravenous feeding, need to be sensitive to other things about living. Most importantly, that it ends in dying. We owe them abundant gratitude for much, but there comes a time to set aside the technology.

I have also signed a document called a power of attorney. This is a vital legal safeguard that means if I am not able to exercise judgement for myself – as the law has it, 'lose capacity' – then individuals whom I trust are empowered to take over. With more people living longer there is an increased incidence of dementia. It might come on slowly, and indeed if identified early enough delaying drugs can sometimes slow the process, but if there comes a point beyond capacity we will each need someone to act on our behalf . . . getting money from the bank, paying bills, cancelling rentals, terminating media contracts and such. Our final months are probably going to be complicated enough for everyone – doctors, carers, family, ourselves – that we can do everyone a service by taking sensible measures now.

The scene in a hospital when someone is on the brink of death is often a tense one. Close relatives and friends will be ushered into a private room; the doctor will come in looking solemn and speaking in a low and gentle voice. You already know what's coming: it will be bad news. But it may be that another – equally quiet and thoughtful – person will arrive soon after. They will ask whether or not you have considered organ donation. This is exactly the most traumatic moment to be asked to consider such a matter. But if the subject has never been raised before then those acting on behalf of transplant medicine will mention it as discreetly as possible. Say 'no' firmly and they will respect your wishes; but you may hesitate, you may pause, you may not say 'no'. You may want to think about it, to know what is involved, to know what good it could do. Your pause could extend a life, restore sight, add active years for someone . . . bestow, for a little while, a kind of immortality.

And then there is medical science.

Outside the school lab there used to be a glass case with bottles of formaldehyde preserving different pieces of human anatomy. We girls were most intrigued by the undeveloped foetus. I very much doubt whether parents or relations had given permission for such use. In former times anything that was not alive was regarded as medical debris and dealt with unceremoniously. More recently, sensibilities have to be considered.

In the autumn of 1999 an almighty scandal hit the headlines. It concerned Alder Hey Children's Hospital in Liverpool which, it was revealed, had between 1988 and 1995 stored body parts from around 850 infants without the knowledge or permission of their families. There was a tide of distress from many parents that led to the setting up of support groups, extended leave for the hospital's chief executive and, after internal and external inquiries, the passing of the Human Tissue Act 2004, which completely revised the former system under which tissue had been retained. I thought back to those jars of yellowing formaldehyde outside my school lab and knew that times had changed.

If you want to donate your body to medical science you have to plan ahead. Bodies have to be donated to specific institutions – hospitals or universities. I think it would be useful if people knew how. So I went to a friend to ask.

Olga's Aunt Iris had been a Land Girl during the war and a farmer in her own right for many years after. By 2006 she was into her nineties and talking of how her body might be 'of some use' to science. Olga resisted the idea . . . perhaps family will. But, under pressure from her aunt, she contacted the Human Anatomy Centre at Cambridge University and spoke to someone called the Bequeathal Secretary, who explained what needed to happen. There were forms to fill in: they needed to know this was Iris's express wish, that she was fully able to make such a decision and that she had signed and had witnessed the appropriate forms. Acceptance of the body when the time came would depend on three things: that she died within a sixty-mile radius of the centre, that they had need of bodies at the time, and that the cause of death – which would have to be certified – would not pose any threat to the students. I imagine similar conditions apply around the country.

Iris Edridge died at six o'clock on a Friday afternoon, about the worst time ever when it comes to getting a death certificate and having it signed by the coroner. The window of opportunity was narrow, and narrowing. But after an almighty fuss of comings and goings the right forms were in the right hands and the Cambridge Anatomy Centre finally took Aunt Iris.

Her body will be with them for about two years. They explained the donation in generously comforting terms: 'She will be the first patient of these medical students and a teacher to them.' At the end of its term of usefulness a committal service is held, at which the students attending speak about the past two years. At that point relatives, though not invited to attend, can send along biographical notes and photographs to give background and reality to the life. The bodies, or what remains, are then cremated and, if so wished, the ashes returned to the family. Aunt Iris will have contributed to the well-being of mankind.

On Money

The winter solstice: the dead heart of the year. From now on the light will grow. The path to the stream is inert and listless, the grass drab, unreached by any step or breeze; it lies in wait for the arrival of longer days. Only the trees have life, the filigree of their branches yielding to a waft of air: there is movement but no joy. Down by the stream there is more movement . . . the water, sluggish and brown, takes its same path round the fallen branch, below the muddy bank, onward to where a shabby rowing boat, unused since the summer, lolls at its place below the owner's garden. I sit on the bench, hugging myself warm with layers of wool. It feels good to be in at the year's turning, the tiny tip of change in the sky, in the light, in the sunlight, hinting at all we want to come. I feel comforted and walk back to the cottage to make tea and light a log fire.

I heft logs from the bin outside the door, scattering shards of bark as I go. The stash of twigs makes good kindling but I take the cowardly route of a firelighter to make sure it flares up. And within minutes the wood is taking on a glow, rewarding my efforts. I fetch tea and a mince pie and settle on the spread of rugs on the sofa. Yes, there is pleasure to be had in the habits of winter, cosying ourselves into nooks of comfort, resolute against the dark outside. I glance through the window panes. It is dark there already, across the grave-yard, the trees shadowy, getting lost in the impending night. It is a long time until spring, but the year has turned the corner.

———

Probably the most conspicuous thing I will leave behind is money. This is not because there is a great deal of it, or even that there is nothing at all. Like many middle-class individuals I shall be leaving a modest accumulation of a lifetime's earning and owning, which in the case of property has enjoyed the unexpected boon of an unsought property bubble. To many, what I will leave will seem a genuine fortune; to others, themselves the inheritors of lavish legacies, mine will seem a puny sum. Before I write my will I must calculate what will be needed to keep me going in my final years when the costs of failing health and competence and the need for personal care will be at their highest. We are warned by actuarial fig-ures and such that most people can expect, on average, two years' dependency. But in individual terms this sum, while important to guess at when formulating some care plan, might be seriously awry. If I step beneath the churning wheels of a belching lorry there will need to be very little deduction made for late-life care. On the other hand, the onset of a slow-moving but inexorably terminal illness will require a rush of available funds and a hollowing-out of whatever expec-tations my inheritors may have. I have warned them as much.

Novels and indeed anecdote tell of families who would prefer the lorry every time.

No, the reason for the focus of my legacy being money is that in our financially obsessed world that is what 'legacy' has come to mean. We make our preferences clear in the wills we write. I speak from the heart of a stable and comfortable setting . . . the envy of many. I can't believe those in Syria's refugee camps or the Dalit peoples hefting baskets of stones by the roadsides of India worry overmuch about who inherits from them. Yet in literature, drama and mythology the formal will and who gets what has come to be a focal point of family narrative. If it deviates in any way from what is seen as 'normal' and 'fair' there are usually consequences.

Jocasta Innes was always clever and inventive; she had been at Girton College in the 1950s when I was at Newnham and even then we recognised an original if wayward spirit. She followed her impulsive nature through several bouts of poverty, writing *The Pauper's Cookbook* – a 1971 bestseller (and still in print) – along the way. Later, she would still be catching the mood ahead of the times with her 1981 design book *Paint Magic*. She had three partners, and four children. She was pragmatic and practical.

When she died in April 2013 her eldest daughter, the successful television producer Daisy Goodwin, discovered she had been largely left out of her mother's will . . . because, as Jocasta had written, 'I think she has less need of it.' It caused immense pain. Eighteen months later Daisy was to write feelingly in the *Sunday Times* about her sense of rejection: 'I am pretty sure . . . she was trying to do the right thing,' but warns that 'maturity dissolves into a puddle of childish resentments. Because when a beloved parent dies what is being parcelled out may look like goods and chattels, but it feels a lot like love.' Response to the article was immediate and abundant, so the paper invited readers to send in their experiences. Many felt as Daisy did, a sense of rejection at the very point when feelings couldn't be mended. 'It felt,' she told me, 'as if my mother had said, "Well, I'll kiss *you*, but I'm not going to kiss *you*."'

There's another reason legacies, wills and inheritance tax have a high profile in our culture. They are the subject of actual state interventions and thus political lobbying, fiscal manipulation, newspaper articles suggesting ways to negotiate your way to a more fruitful outcome . . . more fruitful for your family, that is, not for the state. When you come to write a will you enter a world ringed around with legal regulations, provisions for dispute resolution, and the possibility of family estrangements and the sudden eruption of greed and jealousies that may have lain dormant for a lifetime. What at the start might feel like the chance to take a blank sheet of paper and leave nice things to those you love can plunge you into a maelstrom of conflicting loyalties. You would be wise to think of *King Lear* as only a mild exaggeration.

I caught an unexpected sideswipe when some time ago I wrote in a newspaper what I thought was a straightforward and reasoned argument in defence of – no, more than that – inheritance tax. The response to my column was explosive, and in some cases abusively expressed – far from what I had thought of as my own moderate and conciliatory tones.

People were furious with me, incensed by my casual remarks, moved to sympathise with the plight of my wretched children and altogether convinced that I would some time soon climb through an upstairs window of their own homes and raid their bulging coffers of jewels and gold. It certainly made me thoughtful: why this passionate attachment to worldly goods at the very moment when life is slipping away and they can offer no bulwark against the inevitability of death?

The case I made was this: the inheritance tax is the one we experience without the pain. We don't personally feel its impact at all because we are dead when it is taken from us. Secondly, much of it can be avoided by our own actions while we are still alive by spending more freely before we die. Both of these remain factually true and to me a sympathetic way of regarding a tax that is now built in to our fiscal system.

But what my article unleashed was a visceral rage that the tax should take from people what they feel they own absolutely, and in the case of many seize property on which they had already paid taxes. The disposal of wealth seems to many the final act of direct control they have over their lives, their achievements and their families. But more than that, it is the gesture by which they leave their presence behind them. It will be for many a record of what their lives were worth: in which case, the bigger the better. It is a final cry of self-expression into the void.

My mother left me her gold watch. It wasn't a dedicated act of bequeathment. She made no will and expected everything she had to be dealt with by my father. He it was who gave me her gold watch. It is of course a wind-up watch dating from her twenty-first birthday. On the back it is engraved 'RB March 23rd 1923'. I have had it cleaned and the cracked face replaced with one of exactly the same design. I have not had it valued. The matter of value doesn't arise because I in turn will pass it to my daughter. At the moment, I wear it for evening occasions, taking care to remember to wind it up and not to overwind. It is pretty but not efficient: we have all got used to digital watches now. What is of interest to me is that my mother, who grew up in a Manchester terrace, the eldest of eight children and out to work at thirteen, was given a gold watch on her twenty-first birthday. How could they afford it? Her father worked as a cooper all his life. His earnings were low enough for Friday night's meal to be delayed until he came home from work with the weekly pay packet.

So how did the economics of this gift work out? Had they saved for many months? Had they subscribed weekly, as many working-class families did, to a Friendly Society as a way of saving? It is unlikely they went into debt for such a gift: it was entirely against their rather stubborn principles. The gold watch sits awkwardly among what we know of working peoples' earnings, rents, expenditure on food and necessities at the time. Its purchase remains a mystery, and all the more deserving to be cherished. I doubt that anything I bestow in my turn could represent so hard-earned and generous a gift.

Light is what winter is about, light and how it is refracted through the thin cloud, the low sun catching the last glint of dead leaves. And then the sudden light-burst of sun on lying snow: a dazzling transformation that lifts the spirits. Only snow can lift the city from its torpor, suddenly silencing the streets and gardens, a momentary stillness before the whoops and glee of children. I feel the torpor invade my bones. Old bones. Bones that feel the cold and cower away from draughts and gusts. It comes as a surprise to see the young leaping and running, cutting through the sharp air with easy limbs. Old limbs grow rigid against the cold, muffled against the threat . . . the weather as threat. I watch the sun rise a little earlier each morning; there is still daylight by half past four. Old heads lift tortoise eyes to mark the changes, hanging hopes on the changing year.

———

I decide to take pleasure in writing my will. I begin by listing all my goods and chattels. Funny word, chattels. It only occurs in life at rites of passage, but even the marriage ceremony prefers worldly goods. Chattels is for the dying.

Its origins are French, thirteenth-century. Also *cattle*, the Norman-Picard version of the same word. Where would we be without Wikipedia, and yet there was a time before . . . when there was no Wikipedia and yet people knew things, lots of things. How did they manage that? I was one of them: I read lots of books and made notes, and kept the notes and went to hear people talk, and made notes and kept the notes. I still have the notes. They are among my chattels.

I seem to have a lot of goods that must count as chattels but which are not worth bequeathing to anyone. I have like many people a house full of stuff that a stranger would regard as in some way representing my taste, or 'saying something about me'. But how did I arrive at this motley collection of furniture, books, pictures, crockery, cutlery, clothes that currently occupies space in my shelves, walls, cupboards and drawers. Somehow they have come to surround me without my ever meaning them to.

Interior designers and the magazines that promote their tastes and inventions tell lies about how we live. They would have us aspire to something that represents a coordinated expression of how we see ourselves. They speak of colour schemes and decor, of coordinates and matching fabrics. And we go along with their game. Yet somehow almost daily we deviate from any utopian dreams we may cherish in our imagination just to meet the very needs of daily living. The book group is coming round and I need small tables where they can put their drinks; my children are bringing my grandchildren for a long weekend: a folding bed will be just the thing; a friend has presented me with a fine print of a view we both love. So among my chattels is a nest of white tables, a folding bed and a landscape print. None of this was intended as any kind of furnishing that might be said to reflect my taste. Any self-respecting designer would have them out at once. Nonetheless they are with me daily, merging virtually unnoticed into the background of my coming or going. They are that part of what we own that accumulates episodically as we go through life. Chattels, indeed.

Added to them are the chattels that have come down to me from my parents: a selection of my father's own paintings, my mother's pottery, and books of sepia photographs of people with names like Amy and Aunty Polly bouncing me in their arms on the steps of a terrace house in Gorton. Whereas owners of stately homes have Gainsboroughs and Sèvres china to pass on to their eager descendants, my children scarcely think of themselves as descendants at all, and will be thrown into spasms of disloyalty when, once I am out of the way, they contemplate the unmemorable memorabilia loaded in tired heaps before them and attempt to convince their own offspring that it is part of a significant family heritage. I feel inclined to cut my losses now and do a deal with Oxfam.

Things get more fun when it comes to leaving presents to friends. I was minded to do this when my friend Diana gave me a small white jug shaped like a fish with its mouth agape. It was, she explained, something her husband George would have liked me to have. George Melly, jazz singer and entertainer extraordinaire, had since his teens been seriously fascinated by the Surrealists. So seriously that he worked for many years in the London Gallery, purchasing for himself works that didn't sell – including one or two impressive paintings by Magritte than now hang in public galleries. He also wrote the biography of E. L. T. Mesens the Surrealist celebrity, now overlooked but whose dissolute company he enjoyed. George was also a dedicated fisherman, making his home at the Scethrog Tower in the Brecon Beacons where the fishing was particularly good and where fellow fishermen were invited along for whatever fishermen do. Jeremy Paxman, who writes books about such things, was once accommodated for the night in a tent in their garden.

Thus did the gift of the white china fish represent for me two aspects of my most complex and brilliant friend: the surreal art, an enthusiasm I share, and fishing, a pursuit that I don't. The fish standing on its tail reminds me of an Ernst painting. The gift had been made in his name in the months after George's death in July 2007. The appropriateness of Diana's choice was typical of her care and judgement about such things. It occurs to me now not to wait that long.

I have been to see *The Jew of Malta*, a raging torrent of a play by Christopher Marlowe which is seen from our perspective as a forerunner of Shakespeare's *Merchant of Venice*. Barabas, the hero/villain of Marlowe's piece, is a merchant of Malta, a Christian island threatened by invasion by the Turks – a Muslim empire. The Christian governor attempts to buy off the invaders with monies levied from the island's Jewish population, a directly racist act that in Barabas's eyes, and possibly Marlowe's too, justifies all that comes after. Which is everything: theft, murder, duels, poisoning, executions, mayhem. It is a boisterous load of theatrical high jinks, with Barabas the Jew willing to kill all including his daughter and a household of nuns to hold on to his precious money. Clearly for Elizabethan audiences it was acceptable and amusing to lampoon and deride Jews as miserly skinflints obsessed with property. Shakespeare's play moves into another gear altogether, ascribing motive and subtlety to Shylock even while he remains obsessed with regaining his debts. I feel uneasy about the stereotyping . . . tolerable to a contemporary theatre-goer only on the tacit understanding with the actors that we don't think or behave like this now.

What strikes home, though, is that the love of money and the pursuit of one's legitimate claims on property is described in both plays as a deplorable trait, especially when it comes to transcend love of country, family, child. Perhaps it has to be so demonised because it echoes an unacknowledged feeling in each of us and the underwriting of many of today's financial obligations – between nations, debtors and speculators.

My own financial history has been pretty puny. But money always mattered: not only could we do with more of it to meet the family's rising expectations – a car, a detached house – but there was always a fear that a wrong move or accident could at any moment take away what we had. Wartime made that palpable. People's homes were being bombed out of existence. It could happen to us.

I grew up cautious . . . but trying to be even-handed. On the mantelpiece of my bedroom were two boxes, one labelled Christian Missionary Society, pressed upon me by my Sunday School, and the other my own red Post Office savings box, shaped like a book with a toothed slit through which money could be put in but not taken out. Access was via a key not in my possession. Given money, as I occasionally was – a florin folded secretly into my palm by a departing uncle – I would have to choose which box to put it in. This was a difficult choice: I wanted the money for myself but feared to be judged greedy by the adults who held the key. An echo of that dilemma sounds fleetingly even today whenever a charity appeal drops onto my desk. Self-interest or philanthropy? So much easier, as with inheritance tax, to leave money to charities in my will.

Throughout my life I have been risk-averse: I lack the instincts of the gambler. I might be the only person to have stayed five days in Las Vegas without putting a single coin in a slot machine. Invited in the 1980s by publishing friends Carmen Callil and Liz Calder to put five hundred pounds in a club they were founding for like-minded people, I demurred. It turned out to be Groucho's, which opened in 1985 with five hundred members but was soon to be the go-to place for artistic and literary folk and, before long, one of the hottest private members' clubs in London. It was sold on in 2001, then again in 2008 and 2015, providing lavish returns for those early investors – who do not include me.

Again, I had been approached in 1981 by a theatre producer I knew who was having difficulty raising money for an off-beat musical experiment in which he had great faith. Would I be willing to help out with £750 support? Again, I considered . . . and refused. It turned out to be *Cats*, the musical by Andrew Lloyd Webber based on T. S. Eliot's poems that became the longest-running West End musical of all time, played in thirty countries and three hundred cities around the world, making some £1.7 billion worldwide, multi-millionaires of its creator and producer and riches for investors. But not for me.

There is a good deal of bogus talk around the getting of money . . . perhaps there always has been. The narrative would have us believe that money is primarily the reward for talent, hard work and enlightened self-interest. In my case, this is far from true. The most valuable thing I own and will leave to my children is my house: it is in London, an attractive Victorian terrace house bought in the 1960s for a matter of thousands and now, over fifty years later, fiscally defined as a mansion. Effort on my part . . . nil. We chose it because it faced green trees and sunlight, had tall windows, high ceilings and enough rooms for the family we were planning to have. Its rise in value is no credit to us, merely the unpredicted vagaries of the property market. No talent or hard work went into its purchase. Its modest upkeep has been sustained by the ongoing earnings of a career as a broadcaster and journalist. Starting out today, I could in no way aspire to what seemed at the time a sound but not extravagant purchase made by two working professionals in their early thirties.

What has changed? The world has changed. Money is clearly far from being the reliable solid security we like to imagine. It can balloon out of all proportion, or be wiped out at the collapse of the banking cabal. It is traded by people we don't know and can't trust but who take a slice from our stack for every transaction they claim to be making in our favour.

Fearful of money and its unpredictability, I have always employed an accountant. In the 1980s she explained that if I set money aside for a pension I got tax concessions. That sounded like easy money to me, so I did it. Then when I hit seventy-five years of age I was told I had to take the pension pot I had steadily accumulated and purchase an annuity with it. No option. Again I obeyed. Since then I have enjoyed a trickle of small sums going each month into my bank account. It will carry on doing so until I die. Though I now have another option. New rules mean I can now reclaim my pension pot – much diminished by years of payouts – and use it as I like. I am holding my fire. I hate the rules changing all the time. I am sure it isn't done in the interest of pensioners: what politician would be so selfless? It is clearly in the interests of financial institutions, pension providers, financial advisers . . . oh, and yes, election votes. It makes me wish I had taken shares in the Groucho Club and *Cats* all along.

And so we come to the whole paradox of wills. How are we to reconcile the wish that has prevailed throughout history and seems still to have strong hold on people's passions – the wish to leave the accumulated wealth of our lives to our direct descendants. How do we reconcile that with the manifest fact that inherited wealth spiralling down the generations leads inexorably to the greatest disparity of human wealth that the world has ever seen, the extremes of which match fantastical wealth against the most abject poverty? The inheritors of the Bransons, the Goodwins, the Abramovichs, will join the Rothschilds and the Grosvenors in moving directly into a world where attitudes to working, jobs and obligations are swayed by their gross unearned wealth. This will buy them power and influence over the lives of millions who don't have such choices.

I am sad to leave to my children a world so conflicted about wealth and its ownership. I would wish them the things in life that don't depend on money: health, friendships, love and an enduring curiosity about the world.

On Values

I wait for spring, wait for the time to pass until the warmth returns. What is this waiting? Nothing more than passing through time. Aimlessly. Willing it to pass more quickly, like a child eager for Christmas. Rushing on towards what comes next . . . until nothing does. Does the year have a purpose? Does nature? Time? I know the answer to all these is no. So why are we so purposeful: eager to tend gardens, organise homes, write books, pass laws, run global companies? What genetic glitch fed this frenzy of intent into our DNA?

And does it mellow with age? I am finding it so, here on the bench by the stream. The seasons offer comfort, even as they come full circle.

It started early, and it was reciprocal. My mother went away and came back with a new baby girl. Out of nowhere – it wasn't a birthday or Christmas – I was presented with a life-size baby doll. I would look after my dolly just as my mother would look after hers. Hers was called a sister, and given a name. Mine must have had a name too but I forget it. Our parallel behaviour became almost too close. Each evening my mother set out a series of objects placed around a large enamel basin: Johnson's baby powder, baby soap, safety pins, gauze nappy, towelling nappy, and what was called a binder. I was provided with the dolly equivalent. And as she bathed and dressed my sister I did the same for my doll. I would follow her exact routine.

So enthusiastic was I to copy my mother that it soon threatened to get out of control. I can recall feeling a sense of urgency that I must make exactly the same moves as she did, even to following the same gestures at the same moment. It was when we both reached for the Johnson's baby powder at the same instant that my father was called in to explain that there were different ways of caring for a baby and I didn't have to do exactly as my mother. Oh really? I thought, as my mother seemed to know beyond challenge the only correct way. Was that not so, then? Could I do things my way after all? This is my first memory of realising that I had autonomy, that although my parents' ways were to be copied as the pattern of desired behaviour I might have my own ways too, without incurring their disapproval.

Where do our values come from? And how can we pass them on? Many years later when I was bathing my own daughter I had total and vivid recall of these times spent with my mother. Certain things were different: the baby bath was plastic, and babies no longer had their navels dressed with cotton wool held in place by a six-inch wide binder wound round their bodies. And I was breastfeeding my baby. I never knew whether my mother breast-fed my sister or not. This she would have done in private and never referred to, almost as though it were rude, like bottoms and lavatories. But maternal care seemed to come naturally, simply by virtue of identifying with and copying her. Other values weren't to be that easy.

I had a firm-handed upbringing. Smacking was a regularly used discipline assumed to be a natural component of parent/child relationships, and a way of instilling correct behaviour. It worked. Like Pavlov's dog I quickly learned what would earn me my parents' approval and what would incur their wrath. I also learned that in the latter case it was still possible to get away with things, provided they didn't find out. So secrecy and, if pushed, denying the offence became a received way of coping with the mysterious judgements of the adult world.

My problem was, no one explained why. Children in those days were not given the painstaking explanations liberal parents a generation later would go in for. So I remained unsure of the hierarchy of wrongs. Picking your nose was wrong, but was it as bad as stealing? Was getting mud on the carpet as bad as murder? The two former misdemeanours happened quite often and incurred quick, sharp clips around the ear. Murder and stealing were in the outside world, which remained a place of mystery and vagueness still to be explored.

Nursery rhymes and fairy tales were an escapist treat. Books were precious objects to be cherished and their illustrated contents considered to bear the wisdom of old and hallowed tales. So Tom, Tom the piper's son who ran away with a pig was soundly beaten for his theft. I never doubted that there were fathers who earned their keep as pipers, nor that a pig might be around for easy snatching. I thought it was odd that Little Jack

Horner sitting in a corner – usually regarded as a punishment for mischief – was then allowed to stick his thumb in a pie and feel good about it. Whoever ate with their thumbs? And wasn't there something distasteful about his boasting?

Bo Peep was clearly negligent as a shepherdess; so too was Little Boy Blue, sleeping under the haystack while the sheep ran wild and the cows were invading the wheatfields . . . children clearly had tasks to fulfil and were expected to complete them without supervision. I took the message to heart.

Fairy tales were even more enthralling because they often featured a young girl – Goldilocks, Snow White, Cinderella, Little Red Riding Hood – with whom I easily identified. Unfortunately they all got themselves into trouble, often by walking off alone into the woods. *Into the Woods* is the title of Stephen Sondheim's 1986 musical take on fairy tales and he is right in his emphasis: the concept of 'the woods' embraces all that is mysterious, beautiful, tempting and threatening. There weren't many woods where I lived, but even wandering among a small grove of saplings I knew you couldn't be sure who might be behind you. I also knew that jumping out from behind a tree was an easy way to give parents a shock. When I first saw the Disney film of *Snow White and the Seven Dwarfs* I screamed out with fear in the cinema as the bending trees reach their branches to catch at her clothing. Even today walking in woods I am inclined to look behind for the stirrings of life, and am relieved to see deer, muntjacs, squirrels and rabbits.

Early images shape our life-long fears. And along the way I was probably unconsciously aware of the housekeeping instincts of Snow White, Gretel and Goldilocks, ready to tidy up the messes left by men. The presence of malign and ill-intending stepmothers, wicked queens, greedy witches and ugly sisters warned me that even family life might not be what it seems. I identified with young girls struggling to get what they wanted . . . whether to go to the ball, find their prince or simply survive the greedy wolf or witch's oven.

Since feminism got under way in the late 1960s there have been many insightful analyses of what myths and fairy tales signify. The gender messages of these tales were lost on me in my young years. But I can see, looking back, how steeped they were in stereotypes of gender, wickedness, danger, dependence, rescue, retribution and triumph. Even Peter Rabbit had to pay for his trespass by losing his coat and shoes and being sent to bed with camomile tea. And Cinderella, a poor girl humiliated and demeaned by the grown-ups, earned by her beauty and goodness all the prizes life had to offer. Who could not dare to hope for as much.

And then came Sunday School. By now I knew about good and evil, and knew too that good came from God and Jesus and bad from the Devil. This was the rough ground plan shared throughout the community in which I grew up. Sunday School was a benign way of telling Bible stories that filled out the Jesus narrative, taught us lots of hymns and included moments when, putting our hands together, we 'said our prayers'. I was never quite sure what 'saying your prayers' meant, other than reciting the routine God bless Mummy, God bless Daddy formula with members of the royal family given pride of place.

Church-going became problematic for me because no one had actually spelled out what people did when, on first arriving in the pews, they knelt to pray. I didn't like to ask, so I used to count. Up to twenty usually did it for the time you were expected to stay on your knees. In my own way I was struggling to make sense of what everyone else seemed already to know.

If values are implicit in any society I was absorbing them fast. Fortunately there was an agreed consensus: parents, teachers, the Church all shared the same outlook and knew why murder was worse than muddy shoes. Soon, I knew too. I had encountered the ten commandments and the seven deadly sins.

What happened next has a dreamlike quality to it. I moved forward through my school days attending Religious Education (RE) lessons, morning assemblies every day and confirmation classes followed by a confirmation ceremony. I should have felt and indeed was steeped in Christian doctrine and faith. I accepted it to be true. But there was a sense in which it slid away even as I was being taught it. Everything about what I was told had the beige colour of genteel fashions of the time, at most the insipid colours of English summer dresses: there was no boldness, no resolution about what I heard.

What I did know was that religion was more than a school subject. I knew it was important because it was taught by the headmistress, the only subject of which she took charge. But there was a double bind to that: first she was not trained to teach it, and being a worldly, jealous and snobbish woman had difficulty conveying any sense of religious sensibility; secondly, as headmistress she was always too busy and either late to come to the class or sent word that we were to read the Bible. When she did turn up she tackled the tough stuff head on: St John's Gospel, Chapter 1 'In the Beginning was the Word, and the Word was with God, and the Word was God . . . ' It was no place to start.

I certainly got to know large parts of the Bible well, the New Testament in particular. But it came as a shock when as an adult I learned of the brutal and remorseless ways of the Old Testament God, and that concubines, miscegenation and general waywardness was often the way of the chosen people. School morning assemblies were altogether more engaging; they have lingered vividly in my mind as a time when as naughty schoolgirls we breached the many treacherous regulations, giggled over our petty punishments and enjoyed hearty singing of familiar hymns. The mood of these assemblies, my comfort in the company of my generation and sense I had of feeling secure within familiar boundaries and common purpose has stayed so powerfully with me that I have described them in both my novels. I keep trying to recreate how it felt, so it must have felt good.

Confirmation into full membership of the Anglican Church felt like little more than a formality. The sequence of early-evening meetings held in the church went down like bland porridge. There was little warmth between our instructor and his shy group of pupils. Only once did I try to break the monotony. I put up my hand and asked, 'How do we know any of this is true?' There was a stunned and embarrassed silence all round and I began to feel foolish and awkward. He must have stammered something about it being in the Bible and handed down by centuries of Christian teaching. But I knew I had made some shameful social gaffe. My fellow students looked sneeringly at me, as though I had displayed symptoms of madness. I withdrew in rejection and shame.

The ceremony turned out well, though: I gave up on the theology and concentrated on the clothes. I wore a new dress made for me by my mother of white silk with a petticoat beneath, a waist-length veil with ribbons that held it in place tied behind my ears, and I carried an ivory-backed prayer book, a gift of my godmother, whom I loved because as a manageress of a wartime NAAFI canteen she would slip us illicit hunks of sliced ham. Stealing? It was no worse than muddy shoes.

The war came crashing into my childhood and gave absolute evidence of what I had so far been merely told. Suddenly noise and flames, people in uniform, urgent instructions to follow, frowns and tears. I was deeply upset to see my grandmother crying. Strange things began to happen: children wearing labels were hawked from door to door in an effort to find them homes. They were alone, far from their mothers. Many of them were crying too. The faces of adults when not marred by tears were tense and serious. It made me uneasy. Once I had had the rudiments of war explained to me – Germans, bad, British good – I escaped into a fantasy world where my friend and I resolved to help the war effort (a phrase we'd picked up from the radio and from posters) by creating and acting out our own conspiratorial stories in which we were always the triumphant heroines. These fantasies meshed satisfactorily with the radio news bulletins whose headlines we absorbed into our plots. I spent those growing years not quite knowing fantasy from reality but I most certainly knew good from bad.

Wars induce simplified values: it helps while you are fighting them not to see the enemy as sensate human beings. Young soldiers, we learned, were toughened in the art of killing by using bags of hay for bayonet practice. But soon it would be people: well, they were the enemy after all. We, stalking German spies in the fields of Cheshire, hid in autumn stooks of farmers' wheat to catch them unawares. Trespass? . . . in a good cause. Gradually I came to know the devious ways of compromise, and the beguiling power of group solidarity.

After the war came the election, another crisis of values. Things resolved themselves quite simply. We were to have a school mini-election so we could learn about democracy, a system unquestioningly accepted as a good thing. The day it was announced the girls in my class huddled in groups whispering their loyalties. 'We're Conservative ... Conservative ... Conservative ... ' went the round of the girls I most admired, the dentist's daughter, the doctor's daughter. I was desperate to belong: 'I'm Conservative too. I am!' I said with that craven eagerness of someone not quite at the inner sanctum of popularity. They gave me an appraising nod. That evening I reported events back home. 'Oh, no, but we're Labour. We're not Conservative at all, we're Labour,' said my father with almost reckless glee. To be mocked by him was infinitely worse than being snubbed by the golden girls. Besides, as far as I could tell my parents had been unwaveringly right about everything and I certainly wanted to be right too.

Back at school I took a brave stand. 'I made a mistake,' I declared. 'I'm Labour. I'm not Conservative at all.' It felt a loud and bold declaration as I said it, but must have been a timid whisper for the fact is no one noticed. Only when the actual election arrived and a Labour landslide swept the country did I appreciate how right my father had been. For many years he continued to do no wrong. Then he turned Tory.

Thus are loyalties formed: within families, tribes, peer groups. I was at the threshold of that era in which so many things change and are challenged. I stood on the brink of serious education and the existential turmoil of adolescence. Values were to be thrown in the air, assessed, explored, abandoned, recovered, adjusted and gradually shaped into what was to become my adult self. A giddy journey full of curiosity, loss, regret, discovery and exhilaration. It was when what values I knew finally evolved into my own.

Even as the fighting went on the coalition government of the Second World War was already shaping departments of state to create a fairer and more benign society. It built on a widespread hope of better things; hope was the prevailing mood. Everyone believed things would get better, so they did. The 1944 Education Act would promote equal opportunity based on ability: I was to benefit directly. The Beveridge Report of 1942 set out to tackle the five giant evils: squalor, ignorance, want, idleness and disease. It would bring into being the National Insurance system and the National Health Service – free medical treatment for everyone. Again I and those around me benefited directly. There was sudden and delighted enthusiasm at being able to go to the doctor's for free. It was obvious that these policies had huge immediate popularity: they seemed to the war-weary and run-down people of the country to offer some sort of ongoing reward for the sacrifices they had made.

The vision embedded in these five years was to resonate for decades: the Labour Party of the day – sweeping into government in 1945 then losing to the Tories in 1951 – had created deep-rooted change that shifted the kind of country we were. Attitudes to wealth, taxation, health, education, the role of the state as acting in the interests of us all, shifted for ever. Institutions like the BBC and the Arts Council, manifestly for the general good, were assumed to have enduring purpose and support.

There was an optimistic spirit abroad that acknowledged that public good and civic responsibility would improve all our lives. These were the values I signed up to and which still command my loyalty. I want those who come after to know that yes, we had the vision and yes, it made a difference.

But the reality would prove tough to deal with: the war had gutted Britain's finances; the Korean War of 1950 savaged them further. The utopian idealism of the early years gave way to party quarrels and divisions. Much of the public, restless under continuing austerity and the persistence of rationing, became fractious and discontented. Keynes came back from Bretton Woods with many of his hopes for the global finances unrealised. Soon there would be disillusion in the air.

I was at school when the Korean War broke out; the sixth form was called into the geography room and told that another major war had begun. The teacher may even have pointed Korea out on one of the thick-textured coloured maps that hung from the ceiling. There was universal dismay. Hadn't we put an end to war for good? Hadn't the men come home and peace been celebrated? Was there to be a going back on all of that? I was genuinely shaken to realise that politics reached beyond Europe and things were complicated out there. The defection in 1951 of the spies Burgess and Maclean to Soviet Russia, so recently one of our closest allies, complicated things further.

Domestically, the post-war consensus lasted until the 1970s. This was a time when people seemed to agree about what mattered; there was a strong sense of civic values. Society should be run according to universal principles: everyone was equally deserving of the vote, healthcare, free education, a decent home, quality facilities like roads, railways, libraries and available power supplies. These were often best provided by the state. But there was also a whole world of business supplying us with goods and services promoted and sold as extensively as we could afford. Houses became affordable if you had a decent job, rents were often controlled and social housing provided by the state for those less well off. Private medicine and private education was there for the rich. Times were steady. Goods were abundant and we could increasingly afford them. New stuff arrived: white goods revolutionised housework; television changed leisure. Wages were steady too; there were plenty of jobs and little inflation. This ran smoothly enough within broad political agreement, the Tories always wanting to extend private enterprise and the left resisting.

The global oil crisis of the 1970s threw all this into turmoil. Faced with sudden change, people became fearful they would lose the good life they had come to enjoy. Hope and civic concern ceased to be the prevailing mood. Unions got greedy for their members. Very greedy. Industries were convulsed by strikes. Working at Granada Television I was part of a hugely successful public service series driven off air by escalating union demands. The impact spread: rubbish in the streets, bodies unburied. It became a battle of wills. In the end the Tories under Mrs Thatcher won. The consensus was over. She stood on the steps of Downing Street quoting St Francis: 'Where there is discord may we bring harmony.' She didn't.

So the era of neo-liberal economics dawned. The prevailing ethic ever since has been individual freedom and competitive self-interest. Business and employment were about rivalry and money. It began the great divergence in wealth between rich and poor.

In the 1950s I had embarked on the economics tripos in the heart of the leading school of economics of its day: the Cambridge School. Its founder Alfred Marshall had been its first professor. His book *Principles of Economics* stood on my shelves along with Adam Smith's *Wealth of*

Nations. Marshall's successor Arthur Cecil Pigou shaped the Cambridge School further. He was still alive in the early 1950s, living at King's College, and would on warm days sit on a deckchair with a rug over his lap on the lawns beside the chapel. I looked upon him with awe: that's actually Pigou himself. The inheritor and genius of the Cambridge School was John Maynard Keynes. He had died in 1946: I missed him by just five years.

I absorbed from this remarkable tradition two things. First, its analysis of money, wages, labour and capital. Keynesian economics was the ruling creed of the day; in the 1970s it would be eclipsed by the free market theories of the Chicago school and the heyday of Mrs Thatcher. More recently, as economists have struggled to explain the banking crisis of 2008, the economic collapse that followed and our sluggish recovery, Keynesian theories have again emerged to be championed by many of the world's most outstanding economists. I am pleased about that.

After Part 1 on economics I switched to the history tripos where I studied economic history under the great Eric Hobsbawm. I came to appreciate that theories of economic life must be rooted in a moral outlook. Keynes thought so; so did Adam Smith. Smith's *Wealth of Nations* has been adopted by the neo-liberals as their justification for an economic hierarchy built on self-interest as man's prime motivation, and rational judgement as the basis for his decisions. But Smith also wrote *The Theory of Moral Sentiments*, which sets out the philosophical background for his economic theories. Its first sentence reads:

How selfish soever man may be supposed, there are evidently some principles in his nature, which interest him in the fortune of others, and render their happiness necessary to him, though he derives nothing from it except the pleasure of seeing it.

I am a great admirer of Adam Smith. In recent years I searched out his grave in the churchyard of the Canongate in Edinburgh and stood in respect for his brilliance and subtlety. He would be shocked at the harsh outcomes that the neo-cons deploy in his name.

His writing brings together the two parallel strands of human behaviour, self-interest and altruism. Today we struggle to find a balance between them. Greed and getting rich have become prime motives in the lives of countries and individuals. Care for others, a sense of community, have slipped down our priorities. Single issues continue to inspire the young – climate change, the environment, the world's biosphere. But we are now more in the grasp of Mammon than at any time I have lived through. Profit is seen to legitimise damaging behaviour; harsh working conditions and economic fallout are tolerated in global factories that abuse their workforce. Economic growth is regarded as our universal purpose. Education is being tailored to meet its need. The concept of choice is elevated beyond its usefulness: many in the world have too much choice, many have none. Efficiency is not what we are here for. At the same time concepts like social justice, duty, responsibility for others are at risk of being judged old-fashioned.

I hope it can't last. With the world's resources now under

severe pressure we face global catastrophe. We need to rethink how we deal with living together on the planet. For quite legitimate reasons of hunger and need millions are on the move. Refugee camps are becoming quasi towns. At the same time those who are safe and secure are slow to care and quick to pull up the drawbridge against strangers. Against such fears a potent nationalism takes root. For ourselves we commend aspiration without quite defining what it means: does it mean doing well for ourselves? But at the expense of others? There is a strong case for saying (*pace* Adam Smith) that we cannot be entirely happy in a society that is unfair and unjust.

Money is too much the only god. I wish people would cherish the inner life more. Their sense of their unique identity, their satisfaction with themselves as they are, their freedom from pressure to follow the herd. I have great faith in human creativity: we can see it clearly enough in each small child. Somewhere in growing up it gets neglected or distorted. But where it has flourished people can find their true selves and learn an understanding of others. It is within the writings of great authors, the music of great composers, the painting and sculpture of great artists that we find serenity and inspiration. We can seek in their vision what it is to be human and what to make of our own few years together on this planet.

———

I've seen it . . . yellow . . . the first of the year. Pale at first with the primroses, then the daffodils in bud still sheathed in bright green, the tips waiting their turn. In town there are early bunches in the shops: noisy, bright bunches shouting the spring into coming. Here in the fields the yellows lurk . . .

paler, not yet forthcoming. But I am impatient for them to be here, for the year to turn. I am hurrying time on. To what end? To my own. But how to slow down the flowers?

I leave the bench. It is raining quite hard by now. The buds are more swollen than ever. Time and the river have moved on. I go back up the path and inside for a cup of tea.

On Loss

The clocks go forward. I have the sense of losing an hour, an hour I can't afford to go missing. And soon I will have another birthday, another measurement of man's time.

But outside the lovely world is going on its way. The first sharp green is shadowing the trees. Things grow again, reaching into the timid sunlight. I feel it in my limbs, creaking as they are, carrying the memory of old walks on the hills, of volley and backhand, of stretching to reach the highest branches . . . all things I still do, but do less. That's how it will be. For the trees and birds too; we come and we go.

———

There is something exhilarating about the call when it comes: 'There's not much time left: come now, if you possibly can.' At once the world shifts. You are entering the bereavement bubble, a place of total focus where all the things that preoccupied you moments before shrink into the shadows. Its impact is physical: the pulse races, palms sweat. I feel guilty saying this, but the body is excited. Why do I feel that is an unacceptable thing to say? Because there is some general expectation that feelings should be only downbeat, sad, gloomy, full of worthy melancholy. Well, there will be time for that later. The moment the news breaks there is stuff to be done: schedules to change, meetings to cancel, bags to pack, trains, cars to arrange, and within it all the brain hurtling around dredging up memories, mixing sudden gulps of guilt with huge gasps of tenderness. Outwardly we move calmly through our day – yes, we'll be missing work, thanks for the sympathy, a nod to acknowledge a friend's smile, the gentle hand on the arm. Inwardly turmoil . . . and anticipation.

Being told that someone you love is dying is the moment you embark on one of life's most significant encounters: the encounter with death. In our daily lives we hardly ever see dead bodies. News broadcasters who report on slaughter and famine have strict rules about what to transmit to the public. I recall a BBC reporter telling of how he captured a moment of death so harrowing he believed transmitting it would rouse a public response powerful enough to 'get something done'. In the event the BBC refused: all he was allowed to show was a stream of blood running down a gutter and into a drain. Similarly, world news organisations refuse to show the brutal beheadings made by extremist groups. Quite rightly this is seen as a further brutalising of the individual's integrity. So we don't bump into death as part of daily life. It has been relegated to certain physical locations – hospitals, mortuaries – and, in parallel, to certain locations within our conscious selves.

The call to the bedside has come twice in my life: to my father's and to my sister's deaths. My mother, dying of leukaemia in a high-tech hospital, died in the night-time. The phone call came the following morning. But I recall the two occasions when I actually got to be there in great detail. Or rather, some things are vividly close up in detail: my sister's manicured fingernails, my father's wisps of white hair. But the surroundings – hospital screens, nurses padding tactfully in the background – are all an unimportant blur. What was happening was there in front of me, the change in the person I loved from being there as a person living, breathing in the world we shared, to simply not being there, being gone, absent, ceased . . . or as the formal word has it, deceased. The moment is incandescent with reality. There is life. There is death. We move from one to the other: one moment there is a breath, then there is no breath. What that person was is no more.

Being there with someone you love who is ceasing to be is a great comfort. They are the most precious moments you will share. Suddenly you can be engulfed by regret. 'Why didn't I ask about . . . ' 'I wanted them to know that . . . ' There is a terrible lesson here, reminding us to do the talking earlier in earlier months, if not years. And yes, I do mean 'Tell us what you did in the war, Daddy.'

As the hours pass there are small ways you can help: using a sponge to keep a mouth moist, squeezing a hand to express . . . well, to express everything. For a while there can be a sort of communication: for my father we would ask a question and then say 'Squeeze once for "yes" and twice for "no".' But the time comes when the squeezing stops.

Even without evident awareness I believe there can be a knowing in the mind of the dying. No one comes back from the dead to tell, of course, so how are we to know what activity persists in the dying brain? In the absence of knowing we can go along with assuming what we most wish to be so. In my father's case, he had been dying of cancer for many weeks. But his first great-grandson was due to be born in the weeks ahead and we were convinced he was holding on for the birth. The child arrived at a hospital in Dorset and within days the parents had bundled him into the car and driven north. By the time they arrived my father had lost the power of speech, but as the small newcomer was placed in his lap there were clear gurgles of joy . . . from them both. The wait had been rewarded. In the days that followed, as I sat beside him I chose the moment to tell him that now his great-grandson was safely arrived he himself could go. 'You've done everything . . . you can, if you want, go now.' He took several deep and final breaths.

But the loss was only just beginning, and there were rituals to help. Organising a funeral is a great displacer of personal grief. There is much to be done: hymns and readings chosen, orders of service, music. It had to be explained to the vicar how our individual religious outlooks didn't quite chime with his evangelical style. But both my father and my sister had held an unquestioning acceptance of the Church of England and seemed to go along with what it stood for. Again, among the questions not asked were matters of actual faith and ideas about life after death. And it was too late now. But thank goodness for all that business. For me, the floodgates burst: not only in late-night tears, but in a stream of garrulous reminiscences, photographs brought out, jokes remembered . . . again, a sort of frantic adrenalin-driven excitement around what was happening. Finally I began to emerge from the bubble.

Loss doesn't go away. It mutates into a deep longing and regret. Six months after my father's death we were on holiday in India. Dining at a hotel in Gwalior, at a table next to us were a father with his two young daughters. The girls – around eight and twelve – were eager and happy, teasing and joking with him. He was evidently proud and loving, occasionally catching their hands, smoothing a cheek, taking pleasure in their young lives. I couldn't take my eyes off them . . . then over the dosas and pickle I started to cry. The sobs got worse; I had to leave the table and retreat to my room. In the months that followed there would be other such moments. Over the decades they dwindled. But my father's panama hat still hangs in the cloakroom and his silk dressing gown lies untouched in a drawer.

There have been other farewells. Alerted to the probability that someone may not have long to live, friends who might have called round only occasionally begin to make more frequent visits. When I called on the *Guardian* journalist Jill Tweedie she was no longer able to walk. She sat on a sofa with a blanket wrapping her legs while friends dispensed tea for us all. Jill complained about no longer being able to do the *Guardian* crossword, which had once been an early-morning hit for her lively brain. She used her failure to measure her decline: it irritated her. She hated knowing that her keen intelligence wasn't working as she wanted it to. Within weeks she checked herself into a hospice.

There have been phone calls. My friend the writer Marghanita Laski, a woman of formidable intelligence and implacable will, developed suddenly in her seventies a crippling condition for which there was no cure, only deterioration. It all happened so quickly there was no time for any calling round. Instead the phone rang: 'I am calling to say goodbye, I can't go on like this: later this week I am checking into the Brompton Hospital where I hope to be given something they call the Brompton cocktail. This time next week I shall be dead. But I wanted to say goodbye.' The sheer courage of the woman took my breath away. I stumbled and muttered. It was essential to say something. I ruminated vaguely about whether there were any consolations in her final days. 'No, none. We always believed in the arts, didn't we?' (She had been the vice-chairwoman of the Arts Council.) 'Well, the arts are no consolation at all. None. Language, fine language . . . now that is a comfort.' Over the years she had contributed some quarter of a million quotations to the *Oxford English Dictionary*.

We talked of language: the King James Bible, what she would like read at her funeral. (Nothing religious: she had been a president of the Humanist Society.) And then the time came to say goodbye. And there is only one way to say it: 'Goodbye.' I thanked her for her friendship and all she had meant in my life . . . and then it was time. 'Goodbye.' 'Goodbye.' I put down the receiver, an old-fashioned black Bakelite one. I stared at it for a good while. I can still see it in my mind's eye. And hear her voice.

———

I go outside to look at the moon: a full moon in a clear sky, drenching the fields and the churchyard in silvery light. Very bright, clear enough to read by. Trees, fields, gardens, stream have a night-time stillness. Yet the hush that lies on them hums with the life that sleeps there. I walk with a townie's tentative steps: might I disturb small creatures? Could I encounter an owl? Out in the sky the spaces reach for ever . . . earth's light pollution and the luminosity of the moon throw the stars into shadow. I stand beside the church feeling what it is to be a speck in the universe. It feels good, consoling. I go indoors aware of my place in the scheme of things.

—

I have an increasing sense of my tribe coming to an end. We constituted what is now called a cohort; the great divide that sets us aside within the population is the fact that we remember the war. There are fewer and fewer who do. And the current wave of national anniversaries drives the fact home. Each year there is a smaller than ever group of veterans – many in wheelchairs – passing the cenotaph on Remembrance Sunday, evidence that there are fewer and fewer people who actually have their own memories to recall. For each landmark – VE Day, VJ Day, Arnhem, the Dieppe Raid – there are whiskery old gentlemen wheeled out to wheeze a few words of pride and loyalty to callow young broadcasters. I myself have done that very thing . . . sitting at the feet of surviving suffragettes, the founder of the Girl Guides and the daughter of General Booth, the founder of the Salvation Army. I have heard the reminiscences of Churchill's cook who stayed at her post at Number 10 throughout the war and only went down to the shelters at his insistence, missing a hit by minutes. I have talked to the artist who founded conceptualism: Marcel Duchamp; the composer who wrote silent music: John Cage. I have heard the memories of the widow of the jazz man Lew Stone, and the woman who shared with her husband Oscar

Deutsch the creation of Odeon cinemas: Oscar Deutsch Entertains Our Nation was the popular tag given to the name of the chain.

At each point I have leaned forward eagerly to hear their reminiscences, believing it is somehow important to catch the stories before they are lost for ever. Now I am the one spinning the stories, reminiscing about the original BBC Television Centre, or seeing Manchester burn in the Blitz, and knowing they are only as truthful and accurate as I want to make them. If written history is a construct of all the tales that have been told, then it is an enterprise fraught with bias and improbability. How can there be such a thing as a true record? I feel for the individuals presiding over such monumental and political acts of recall as the Saville Inquiry into Ireland's Bloody Sunday, the Chilcot Inquiry and Dame Janet Smith's review for the BBC of its culture during the Jimmy Savile years. Who to believe, who to record. The role of historian is indeed a noble calling.

But our loss does not go unremarked. These days I turn to the newspaper obituaries with the same sense of involvement as when younger people turn to sport. Who will have gone today? It is rare that my fears are disappointed. And there they go . . . the parade of my contemporaries, some younger, some older, stepping on to that conveyor belt from earth to heaven that Powell and Pressburger invented for *A Matter of Life and Death*. Their passing defines my place on that same conveyor belt. I am just not there yet. But already ahead of me are friends and colleagues, people I have interviewed, people not known personally but admired. These are not all intimate losses, though some may be. The fact their deaths are recorded

in the newspapers indicates they meant something in the life
and culture of the country. They often represent the best of
what we were. Within barely more than a twelvemonth I read
with sorrow of those whom I had known:

Musicians John Tavener, Christopher Hogwood, John
Shirley-Quirk; artists Albert Irvin, Alan Davie. From the
world of writing: Elizabeth Jane Howard, Richard Hoggart
and his journalist son Simon, Karl Miller, Jon Stallworthy,
Dannie Abse, Deborah Rogers, Martyn Goff. From television:
Richard Kershaw, David Lomax, Michael Kustow, Daniel
Topolski; actors Roger Lloyd-Pack, Rik Mayall and Richard
Pasco; film-maker Richard Attenborough. Movers and shak-
ers: Michael Birkett, Ben Whitaker, Deborah Mitford, Helen
Bamber. My life has been richer for having them in it. And
poorer without.

> They are all gone into the world of light!
>   And I alone sit ling'ring here;
> Their very memory is fair and bright,
>   And my sad thoughts doth clear.
>
>   Henry Vaughan

On Death

I dreamt last night that they were destroying my home: taking it apart, heaving stuff out and breaking up shelves. I was there in the picture, trying to stop them but they couldn't hear me. They went on regardless of my shouting, my plucking at their clothes. I was distraught. They went on, clawing at the garden, tearing down the hedge of roses, swinging the five-bar gate off its hinges. I struggled with them without their responding, trying pathetically to tie the flowers back along the fence, hoping to retrieve something from their damage. What's strange is that it wasn't the house I actually live in: it was a house I loved and left some twelve years ago, a country retreat lost to change and divorce. There had been newcomers there long since, so I couldn't imagine what tricks my imagination, my subconscious was playing. But clearly my distress was overwhelming. I woke in a sweat, my heart pounding, shook myself and went for a brisk walk round the bedroom, relocating myself in the present . . . the nice cosy comfortable present.

Of course, that is where we all long to be, the comfy

present, though we don't often think about it; taking it for granted as the very given of existence, never recognising the fact that it is miraculous we should be here in a specific place on the planet at a particular moment in time. We never give it a moment's thought. Students of mindfulness say we should be in the present, live knowing the moment. Anything would be better than my nightmare and my place in it.

The cacophony of birdsong wakes me early. Relieved, I throw the windows open wide and lie in the big soft bed. The sounds soar in the air; ricocheting from the church wall on the far side of the graveyard, flocks of linnets congregating in the bushes. The sound of frantic activity. Later, walking, I see a blackbird pair, he black with the bold yellow beak, she brown and nondescript: they each have grass in their beaks. Being a city-dweller I don't know where to look for the nest. On the river two Canada geese land suddenly from nowhere. They seem cumbersome beside the delicate precision of the local birds. I feel cumbersome too, an outsider come to nest again in this gentle spot. But there is life stirring. And in me too. The golden cycle of the year . . . of my years.

I think my nightmare was in some small way a presentiment of my death. I have them more and more often. As the calendar of weddings has given way to the calendar of funerals it is impossible not to notice that on my way along the path of life I am in sight of the end. I've asked others in their eighties and they say the same. 'I think about death every day,' the writer Howard Jacobson said when he was only seventy-two.

I try to recall what it was like not to be aware of death, how carefree and upbeat that must have been. I hope it might be possible. Just as at the sound of certain music – Dylan's 'Blowin' in the Wind', say, or the Beatles' 'Hey Jude' – my mind suddenly switches back into that era and for a moment . . . even as much as minutes together I have not only total recall of those times but experience within myself what it felt like to be me then. I get a rare and unexpected – it's always unexpected – flavour of those times and my times in them. I would like, on the same basis, to recapture the sense of the world stretching out ahead for ever, an unquestioning expanse of hope and expectations.

Hopes and expectations have dwindled now: there is not as much time ahead to look forward to. How could it be otherwise? The question is how to deal with it. For many of us there's the temptation to slump into despair, made even worse if you're recently bereaved and alone for the first time in a long while. In a sense that is the easy, undemanding path to take. Depression certainly comes almost naturally to the old.

Making *Inside the Ethics Committee*, the issue came up of an old person who had a long and lingering illness, and her expressed wish to stop the medical intervention that was keeping her alive. Concern was expressed by some of the medical staff that she might feel that way because she was depressed and that they should consider treating her depression with medication. I was amazed. It seemed natural to me that she was depressed: she had an illness from which she would not recover and she was not far from her death. The problem is that in some cases the word depression has been stolen by the medical absolutists who regard it as a specific mental condition. And therefore treatable. Whereas in the real world it is a human condition. And it is unconsolable. I prefer to call it melancholy.

The novelist Kingsley Amis was a neighbour and acquaintance of mine; we shared the same birthday and on that occasion I would sometimes go round to raise a glass. I know he enjoyed my company but was unimpressed by my intellect. He made that clear. His was an extraordinarily diverse character: he could be very dark and fearful, dreading the dark and being alone. On those occasions he was like a small boy needing, but not asking for, comfort and sympathy. At other times he was hugely entertaining, throwing himself into the pleasure of being the centre of the crowd, keeping us in continuous laughter as the most brilliant mimic of mutual enemies . . . and friends. The year he won the Booker Prize for *The Old Devils*, he made no secret of being overjoyed, and issued lapel pins declaring 'I won the Booker Prize'. These were handed to friends to wear at the small lunch party that followed. There was plenty of laughter and champagne and again a sense of the small boy, this time triumphant.

In 2004, almost ten years after his death, his biographer Zachary Leader came across an unpublished poem. You may wonder why it took so long, but the Kingsley Amis archive at an American university consists of sixty-eight boxes of papers. The poem is stark and poignant, stripped of any of Amis's irony or judgement. It is direct and honest and speaks to us all:

Things tell less and less:
The news impersonal
And from afar; no book
Worth wrenching off the shelf.
Liquor brings dizziness
And food discomfort; all
Music sounds thin and tired,
And what picture could earn a look?
The self drowses in the self
Beyond hope of a visitor.
Desire and those desired
Fade, and no matter:
Memories in decay
Annihilate the day.
There once was an answer:
Up at the stroke of seven,
A turn round the garden
(Breathing deep and slow),
Then work, never mind what,
How small, provided that
It serves another's good.
But once is long ago
And, tell me, how could
Such an answer be less than wrong,
Be right all along?
Vain echoes, desist.

This is a poem of utter despair. For those of us still glad
to have the morning, the turn round the garden, the work,
it seems bleak indeed. Except for one thing: Kingsley Amis

did write the poem. He still sought to express himself, still sending out into the world his view of it, sharing the words others would read. But clearly not for long.

So how can we best face the fact of our coming death? It is of course a universal problem: I recall being in despair at the fact of death in my teens. On New Year's Eve, with parents out celebrating, I would watch the mantelpiece clock ticking the seconds away towards the next year. I had an intense sense of watching time pass with each tick of the second hand, one year passing into history, time moving on, and I was helpless to stop the clock. I remember crying out in anguish to the silent house and a sister asleep upstairs, 'Oh, no, no, no.' That helplessness felt primordial. Then as I grew up some mechanism of the human psyche intervened to make living possible. There must be the equivalent of a filter that cuts out the raw and unavoidable truth. But the filter wears thin as friends and colleagues die; I find it needs a conscious act of will to live in the present. I exercise this particularly at dawn, drawing back the curtains and looking out upon trees and the growing light. In that moment I have learned to relish the prospect of another day, and another, coming along in so far unthreatening succession. Each day is after all as long – a full twenty-four hours, each hour sixty delicious minutes – as a day is long when you are younger. But we take time at a different pace as we get older. How reckless it was to toss days away as if there were plenty more to come . . . simply because there were plenty more to come.

The procedures of death are no longer secret. They are being brought out into the open, shaken free of archaisms and obscurities and made answerable to the needs of the bereaved and the wishes of the dead. My memories of early loss, grand-parents, remote relations, are of some blanket of secrecy and even shame. It was spoken of in whispers and behind cupped hands. Illnesses were disguised in code: cancer was the Big C, a whole clutch of unspeakables were lumped together as 'women's problems'. In our corner of the Church of England bodies were left at the undertaker's until leaving there for the funeral: viewing of the body was seen to be unhealthily morbid. There was discussion as to at what age and degree of closeness children should be allowed to the funeral. As the hearse proceeded through the streets, followed by carloads of mourners, traffic would respectfully come to a halt, and the curtains of windows along the street be drawn as a mark of respect. Rituals of behaviour and dress were strictly formal: the standard C of E service before a congregation in black clothes, the women always in hats. Interment was favoured; cremation was seen as somehow new-fangled and ruling out the outside chance of a bodily resurrection.

As with everything else, patterns are changing, bring-ing in more diverse ways of behaving, allowing departure from tradition. So which will it be? A cardboard coffin with scribbled messages from the grandchildren, a wicker-work coffin paying regard to the environment to be interred in a forest, perhaps, or even your garden? Or will it be reduction to ashes, to be kept in an urn displayed on the mantelpiece or hidden in the cupboard under the stairs. You could leave instructions that you want to be scattered: I know of some-one who took their partner's ashes to the Caribbean where she went diving with the urn and opened it under water, letting the dust drift dramatically away into seas where they had once swum together. There is a danger in opting for your own garden, under a weeping willow, beside a favourite rose tree, because when the house goes up for sale your dust will be left behind in the indifferent charge of someone who could drive a plough through your flowerbed or dig you over to make a pond.

All this only matters if you have some sense that your bodily remains represent something important of yourself. I don't. I believe that in the long run, given millennia and a future for the cosmos, that as the song says 'we are stardust'. I have left instructions that, having yielded up any useful parts of my body for transplants, I will be cremated and my ashes scattered on the River Cam in Cambridge, the city where my whole life shifted focus, where I learned what life held in store and where I fell in love – not only with individuals but, more consistently, with the life of ideas.

With traditional ritual often abandoned, the event of a funeral takes on its own character. Families and friends take part, young children singing songs or playing instruments. The selection of music is for the bereaved to choose and in recent years they've been letting rip. Unconstrained by fear of judgement day, and wary of expectations beyond the grave, a great many people opt for what they know in the world of today. That means television theme tunes, football anthems and popular songs. Among the most popular is the hit song from Monty Python's *Life of Brian*, 'Always Look on the Bright Side of Life'. Played at an actual funeral it must seem odd, reflecting an uneasy jocularity about death while being intent on suppressing grief. A comic film, yes, but a funeral?

A favourite for a long time was Frank Sinatra singing 'My Way' . . . again another defiant shout in the face of the inevitable. Others include 'You'll Never Walk Alone', 'You Raise Me Up', 'Somewhere Over the Rainbow' and the love theme from the film *Titanic*, 'My Heart Will Go On'. They all manage, in a rather soupy way, to suggest some ideal future where love endures and friendships continue. I am comforted to know that remaining in the list of funeral favourites are 'Abide with Me', 'The Lord is my Shepherd' and 'Ave Maria', good old reliable choices that at least vaguely touch on religious sentiment.

And yet I'm being hypocritical here because I know when I roll this question round in my head about my own funeral I come up with the Beatles – 'In My Life', possibly or George Harrison's 'Here Comes the Sun'.

And then there are the memorials. Following the funeral, often months later. Memorials are the new parties, reflecting the shift from religious concerns to celebration of the life of the deceased. As the years go by I go to more and more of them. They can be really large-scale events, planned and choreographed with love and care for the dead always in mind. Some approach pageants in scale: Mary Soames, Winston Churchill's last surviving child, had trumpeters of the Household Cavalry Band, and 'The Battle Hymn of the Republic'; Alan Coren had the last page of *The Great Gatsby*; David Frost had a reel/montage of his programmes, and the unveiling of a memorial stone in Westminster Abbey. Composer Sir John Tavener's memorial included his own music – spiritual rather than religious – played by the Britten Sinfonia and by the cellist Steven Isserlis. Always there are readings and tributes by friends: at Richard Attenborough's memorial Sir Ben Kingsley and Geraldine James read from the writings of Gandhi. These were all grand occasions, but those celebrating friends are if anything more moving. To hear the novelist Andrew O'Hagan speak of his debt to his editor and literary guru Karl Miller was to learn more of the intelligence and affection of each; to hear Valerie Grove speak of her Cambridge friendship with Simon Hoggart was to share again the mood of laughter that always surrounded him. Ned Sherrin, producer and creator of *That Was The Week That Was*, once wrote reviews of funerals and memorials for the *Oldie* magazine. They were fun to read. Certainly such neo-theatrical events deserve to be appreciated well beyond the crowds that fill the pews. I think we can expect more of them.

But there was one I missed. I understand the memorial to Harold Pinter filled the 1150 seats of the Olivier Theatre: actors, playwrights, producers, literary figures, journalists and of course family and friends. It was a grand event with readings from his work by among others Eileen Atkins, Colin Firth and Penelope Wilton. But I missed it all. What happened was this: some ten days before I had a phone call from a friend. Could he come round? He had something important to discuss. Odd. I was completely unsuspecting of what he was about to say. He arrived, and was distinctly uneasy. It was soon clear why. He had been deputed via a series of friends to convey a message to me: Antonia Fraser would like me to stay away from Harold's memorial.

Harold had died on Christmas Eve 2008. Mine must have been one of an avalanche of condolence letters sent to his widow. I knew the family funeral would be private; of course it must. Our mutual friend Henry Woolf would be among the mourners and I asked that he let me see his copy of the order of service. Which he did. There would be time enough for me to make my farewells at the much larger and therefore more anonymous memorial event. I had in a sense been saving my grief until then. That was why the request came as such a shock.

I discussed my quandary with many friends, in the theatre world and beyond. How should I feel? How to respond? My feistier girlfriends' advice was 'Go anyway! Just refuse her request!' Others were more temperate: 'It isn't usual for the mistress to go' was one unsoothing comment. But others told of many instances where former girlfriends and lovers had indeed turned up to mourn the man they had all loved.

In the end I did nothing. I left the diary blank for that day – 7 June 2009 – and spent it remembering Harold in private. After all, that was how I had known him most intimately and where my most cherished memories lived.

In recent decades my life has moved in many emotional directions; in my eighties it has come into relative calm. That isn't to say I don't need, and welcome, attention, friendship and love. There is scarcely anyone alive who does not. But I live contentedly alone – it's better that way – and am often thoughtful about what has been and what might have been. There are many like me. My friends, too, often live on their own. We depend increasingly on each other for the bonds of affection, and in some circumstances comforting jars of honey and visits to hospital. We are lucky: we have homes and comfort and enough savings for what we need. These are the networks of the old: you see us in restaurants, cinema queues, art galleries, small hotels and occasionally on cruises. We meet over dinner, we belong to book groups. Some of us enjoy gardening, swopping cuttings, arranging flowers. We cook. We remember birthdays and reminisce. We share news of our children, our ailments, the latest online shopping, our hardening political views, our views of books and plays, music and art . . . And, yes, we discuss and elaborate our plans for the future. We are content.

For us the seasons become more meaningful: old bones feel the cold. I am glad winter is passing. But there is still February, the most treacherous month. Not a time to be out and about, not a time to be at the cottage. A time to be in the sun: the Bahamas, the Canaries . . . exotic islands. The city's spirit is damp, like its streets. I relish the newly arriving spring.

His name is Henry Wadsworth Longfellow, a popular American poet whose *Hiawatha* was part of many a childhood, including mine. Its unfamiliar rhythm suggested that he had private access to the speech patterns of American Indians but the idea has been much called into question since.

The poem is called 'A Psalm of Life'. It has famous lines in it but is not itself famous.

There are nine verses and the one of which you have a dim recollection is probably this:

Lives of great men all remind us
We can make our lives sublime,

And, departing, leave behind us
    Footprints on the sands of time;

As a proposition it doesn't bear a moment's examination.
The lives of great men remind us of many things: how inef-
fective we are in comparison, how (if you're a woman) only
men get the chance to shine. How tough it is at the top; how
influence and money win the day. But not that 'we can make
our lives sublime'. What does that mean anyway? What is a
sublime life? Is it a very happy one, in which we can enjoy a
life away from the hurly-burly of great men, nestling within
our own little family, possibly within a thatched cottage with
roses round the door? All sublime of course; there's probably a rose called 'Sublime'. Or is a sublime life one in which
we triumph over adversity and our adversaries? Was Helen
Keller's life sublime? And Napoleon's? What about Stalin?
And Herod? Mother Teresa? You can trawl through history
in search of the sublime life and still not come up with one
truly sublime enough to qualify. Not as an exemplar to ourselves, that is.

I am persuaded Mr Longfellow (it was characteristic of
F. R. Leavis to refer to those he disapproved of as Mr: I once
heard him lecture on Mr Auden, so Mr Longfellow) was in all
probability looking for a rhyme for 'time'. And in that respect
he was entirely successful.

There are other remembered lines too, even though they
are not strictly memorable. 'Life is real! Life is earnest!', 'Art
is long and Time is fleeting'.

These are not his own, but appropriated in the interest of
high-Victorian polemic:

> In the world's broad field of battle,
>   In the bivouac of Life,
> Be not like dumb, driven cattle!
>   Be a hero in the strife!

So there you have it: the world is a battlefield and we are camped in the middle of it, playing dumb but urged to be a hero. There's an abundance of exclamation marks, which means, I think, that Mr Longfellow believes these to be high – if not sublime – sentiments. But there is worse to follow. After we have left our footsteps in the sand then someone else – a shipwrecked brother – will fetch up on the shore and, 'Seeing, shall take heart again'. There is a problem with this metaphor. Always supposing a beach and a shoreline and footsteps printed thereon, won't the tide come in and wash them away? Unless the shipwrecked brother is hot on your heels before high tide he has no chance of being inspired by your footsteps to take heart again. This is the old Man Friday problem. Footsteps imprinted on sand must by definition be recent.

In conclusion. This is a terrible poem, born of false sentiments and careless writing. But it has a saving grace. By some accident of poesy it has left us with a concept that we want to believe in . . . that we can leave footsteps behind us when we die so that those who come after can remember we lived and consider how the world changed while we were alive. It is an idea I have been trying to trace in these pages.

———

'I wasted time, and now doth time waste me.'

Shakespeare, *Richard II*

'Time is of the Essence, so which quick and tasty dinner will
you be tucking into tonight?'

The Co-operative Food Twitter

Down by the river the dandelion field is in full bloom again.
The dandelion clocks will come.

Acknowledgements

This book was made possible by the generous help of many people. Primarily I must thank the Hosking Houses Trust, which made available their very special place where I could retreat and think and write. Sarah Hosking – founder and sustainer of the charity – was a friend at all times.

To my inspirational editor Lennie Goodings I owe a debt as big as ever. This book wouldn't have happened without her, and her team at Virago, Zoe Gullen and Zoe Hood. My agent Ed Victor was his usual continuing strength.

Others have offered me their diverse skills and friendship: Andrew O'Hagan, Diana Melly, Ernie Eban, Olga Edridge, Damien Hirst, Michael Craig-Martin, David Steele, Carmen Callil, Laurence and Brigitte Marks, and Frances McCarthy. My children, Harriet and Matthew, have given loyal encouragement throughout.

Credits

99   Extract from Judith Flanders, *The Making of Home: The 500-Year Story of How Our Houses Became Homes* (London: Atlantic, 2014).

133–4   Extract from *The Waste Land* taken from *Collected Poems 1909–1962* by T. S. Eliot © Estate of T. S. Eliot and reprinted by permission of Faber and Faber Ltd.

151   Lyrics from 'Five Minutes More'. Music by Jule Styne, lyrics by Sammy Cahn. Copyright © Morley Music Co.

157   Extract from 'Annus Mirabilis' taken from *The Collected Poems* by Philip Larkin © Estate of Philip Larkin and reprinted by permission of Faber and Faber Ltd.

170   Lyrics from 'Blurred Lines' by Pharrell Williams, Clifford Harris and Robin Thicke. Lyrics © Sony/ATV Music Publishing LLC.

173   Extract from 'The Dance' taken from *Collected Poems* by R. S. Thomas. © R. S. Thomas, 1993. Reprinted with permission of the Orion Publishing Group, London.

207–8   Oona King, 'Benedict Cumberbatch is right', *Independent*, 3 February 2015.

224   Extract from 'Whispers of Immortality' taken from *Collected Poems 1909–1962* by T. S. Eliot © Estate of T. S. Eliot and reprinted by permission of Faber and Faber Ltd.

225   Extract from 'Aubade' taken from *The Collected Poems* by Philip Larkin © Estate of Philip Larkin and reprinted by permission of Faber and Faber Ltd.

282   Things tell less and less by Kingsley Amis. Copyright © 2004, The Estate of Kingsley Amis, used by permission of The Wylie Agency (UK) Limited.

Picture Credits

© Damien Hirst and Science Ltd. All rights reserved, DACS 2015. Photo: André Morin-Le-Jeune: 226
© Tate: 230
Tim Gidal/Getty Images: 264